M-8
Price, $3.00

SOCIAL RESEARCH CONSULTATION

—An Experiment in Health and Welfare Planning

By

ROLAND L. WARREN

RUSSELL SAGE FOUNDATION

New York   1963

HV
88
.N78
W3

Contents

3

From the Agency Administrator's Viewpoint

Introductory Comments

By

GORDON E. BROWN

Executive Director, State Charities Aid Association

In the main part of this volume, Dr. Roland L. Warren recounts the successes and difficulties encountered in the experimental introduction of a social science research service into an ongoing health and welfare agency. These few pages will tell how the administrative head of that agency views the experience.

THE SOCIAL RESEARCH SERVICE of the State Charities Aid Association was begun as a demonstration; it now has been made a permanent part of the Association's program. If action reaches beyond words, no further documentation is needed to show that it has proved to be a strong resource for sound performance in the health and welfare field.

But as Dr. Warren points out, this is only an indicator of the success of the project. More directly, the administrator found the social research worker helping him practice the art of getting something done through first satisfying his conscience and constituency that the "something" really needed doing. The scientific approach enabled more precise determination of the nature of health and social problems and how to attack them.

The State Charities Aid Association is a voluntary organization, founded ninety years ago by private citizens to aid what was then known as the New York State Board of Charities. The goal was social reform. Today the central purpose remains the same:

working with government—and with other voluntary groups—
for the improvement of health and welfare conditions throughout
the state. From the outset of this demonstration, therefore, its
influence on governmental as well as private endeavors was considered important.

The Association's expectations went beyond the immediate
episodes of research in program planning by the agencies receiving its behavioral scientist's consultation. It also anticipated that
in receiving assistance these groups would become persuaded of
the intrinsic soundness of using the scientific method. Dr. Warren's report is another step in furthering such hopes.

Social research, of course, is not the chief function of the State
Charities Aid Association—nor are its other activities in public
relations, fund-raising, or business management, for instance. All
are instruments for serving the communities of New York State.

The Association works at both the local and state levels.
Locally it informs and advises with community health and welfare agencies—such as public welfare departments, health departments, mental health boards, voluntary health associations,
hospitals, health and social planning councils, voluntary welfare
groups, and the like. At the state level it works with the legisla-
ture, with state administrative departments (especially Health,
Welfare, Mental Hygiene, and Education), and with statewide
voluntary organizations. The state activities, however, aim ultimately at meeting local health and welfare needs through improved laws and state agency assistance.

At both levels the Social Research Service made important
contributions. When the social research director aided either a
local or state group he furthered SCAA's community-serving
purpose. Specifically, his work (1) improved and increased the
help to be given these groups directly, and (2) enabled effective
planning of SCAA's activities in general—again, through greater
understanding of the health and welfare problems that demanded
attention.

An example of the former was the designing of surveys through
which voluntary mental health associations assessed community
mental health needs; of the latter, a statewide inquiry among

community leaders to find what they felt were high-priority local problems. Results from this inquiry led the SCAA to establish an additional program to advise groups on developing resources for chronically disabled persons. In fact, the way in which the Social Research Service had so well fitted into the structure of the SCAA showed how the new chronic disability unit might be organized.

Dr. Warren's report, in the tradition of objective science, records failures as well as achievements. It voices occasional disappointment, and for some of this the SCAA administrator must be held accountable. There were times, too, when staff members unwisely sought to exploit the social research director's talents in tasks that might more properly have been assigned to others. But this happened infrequently because in concert with the administrator Dr. Warren had well outlined his functions at the outset.

Although the behavioral scientist can strengthen the administrator's hand in adjusting the agency's program to changing social conditions, he cannot be expected to provide formulas for action. He is supportive, not substitutive—the administrator still must make the final decisions, and almost always on the basis of less information than, ideally, he would like to have. But the social research worker can be an invaluable guide for the administrator who seeks tangible grounds for his course of action.

What are some of the reasons for this happy marriage of social science and social practice?

Above all, the Association started with sufficient grasp of what social research entails to envision how it could help in appreciating the social aspects of human behavior.

To direct the project a behavioral scientist was required rather than, for example, an epidemiologist, a statistician, or a social or public health worker with research experience. He would be a full-time member of the staff rather than a part-time consultant, even though an *ad hoc* arrangement might be satisfactory for many agencies. Dr. Warren's account will be as pertinent for these groups as for those that may fully employ a social researcher now or in the future, for most of his work took the form of *ad hoc* consultation to state and local agencies.

The Association was fortunate in getting the right man to direct the new program. Dr. Warren brought skilled and vigorous leadership. As he notes in his report, he was already familiar with the agency, having served as a volunteer on the Board of Managers and various committees of the Association. This was obviously an advantage, but not essential.

Today health and welfare organizations are being increasingly—and properly—held accountable by the public. To wish to do good is no longer sufficient for citizens who provide support through taxes, gifts, or voluntary services. The agencies also must do well. The public expects public service organizations, voluntary or official, to remain sensitive to the needs that exist in fact and not simply in their minds.

In its behavioral scientist the Association soon found it had someone to remind it of these obligations. He would ask, for example, whether its work really exercised impact on those it should be serving. This can be disconcerting and challenging— especially for an administrator. Yet, as Dr. Warren observes, social research must concern itself directly with the agency's effect on those it purports to benefit. To know whether the organization is following accepted professional standards—important as that may be—is not enough.

Vital to the success of this demonstration was the breadth of Dr. Warren's concept of his role. He often felt responsibility for going beyond the stage of designing studies, even entering the phase of action when appropriate. Thus he used his influence to encourage sound implementation. But were he ever charged with overreaching the acceptable role for a behavioral scientist, the Association did not hear it.

Another element in this favorable experience was that the social research director served as a member of the administrative team, which numbered nine professionals at the project's start. It is not surprising that Dr. Warren lists this among his four main functions (along with encouragement of research, consultation on projects, and interpretation of scientific method and findings). His place on the team was essential to dovetailing his activities with the overall work of the agency.

The social research director also contributed not only as a behavioral scientist but as a mature adviser in matters outside his profession. A social investigator's training, Dr. Warren points out, predisposes him toward analytical detachment, whether consulting specifically on study plans or voicing less specialized opinions on the agency's work. The Association found its behavioral scientist exerting a leavening influence during group considerations that led to decision-making. He helped to span the gaps in point of view between members of different professional disciplines, between the layman and the professional, and between the private citizen and government official.

As social research enables better agency performance, the administrator may take such satisfaction in this progress that he wants to do an even better job. At the very least the experience recorded here has demonstrated for this agency how the scientific method can help instill the confidence derived from having well-defined destinations, with well-marked directions for getting there.

1. The Project and Its Setting

As SCIENTISTS in any field apply the knowledge and techniques of their disciplines it is highly desirable that they record their experiences. In this way a body of principles develops to guide future practice. But it is especially appropriate for behavioral scientists to do so, for their activities necessarily involve larger institutional contexts and social processes that become the data for further study.

Among the barriers to the construction of a sound body of principles in applied fields is the preoccupation of practitioners with what has happened among the social units they are working with, while little attention is given to what they themselves have done to influence the process. The detached "pure" research investigator understandably seeks to make the effects of his own intervention minimal. But the applied scientist is attempting not only to learn, but to bring about some change. In so doing he is drawn into the social world he is observing, and his own actions implicitly become part of the social facts in the case.

There is consequently a need in applied social research not simply to report what happens but to analyze what happens as a result of the behavior of the practitioner. This book seeks to do this in connection with a three-year demonstration of social research consultation with voluntary citizens' groups.

The venture was based upon the assumption that with the help of a social scientist these organizations could study to better advantage the community situations they were trying to improve, have access to knowledge already available from the behavioral sciences, and so perform their avowed functions more effectively.

Following this general assumption, a variety of consultation episodes took place. Although a tentative policy was developed at the outset, and although there was considerable analogous experience to guide the demonstration, much of it took place through "playing by ear." Let us be frank to concede that some decisions were made rather deliberately on the basis of "hunches." But throughout the process, an attempt was made to plan, to observe, to understand, and to modify. If we were playing by ear, we were also trying to get some of the harmonic structure of the sound on paper; looking for regularities of sequence and for concepts to describe them by which we could communicate what had been learned in a manner to facilitate application to other similar but not identical situations.

We shall try not to make this simply a "how we did it" book. We shall attempt, rather, to relate the events that occurred in terms of concepts from the behavioral sciences, so that the account may be read against a background of what is known in those disciplines. Further, we shall seek principles behind the events to serve as tentative guidelines for future practice while being tested by experience.

The data for this analysis consist of thirty instances of research consultation service to voluntary citizens' groups in the health and welfare field in New York State. Some were on the city and county levels, and some were with state-level parent organizations. The projects varied tremendously in extensiveness, in the timing and amount of research consultation, the source of initiative, the success or failure of the effort as a research project, the impact on the organization that conducted or sponsored it, and the utilization or nonutilization of the findings in making program changes. They varied from relatively simple "fact-finding" projects, conducted by laymen with a minimum of professional guidance, to rather sophisticated projects with professional research staff.

A systematic analysis of these episodes may thus be of value not only to social scientists and others who offer research consultation, but to local organizations that utilize consultant services, and to state or national voluntary organizations that may be considering consultation service for their local affiliates. The account also has relevance for governmental agencies since public as well as private agencies participated in the projects described.

Background

The consultation service reported here is an outgrowth of Russell Sage Foundation's program of promoting more effective working relationships between the behavioral sciences and various fields of professional practice.

It so happened that the State Charities Aid Association of New York several years ago was considering the introduction of a service through which its many and varied affiliates might evaluate the effectiveness of their programs. This organization is the oldest and perhaps the most widely known statewide citizens' organization in the field of health and welfare. It has a unique combination of state level affiliates and respective local citizens' organizations. These include the State Committee on Tuberculosis and Public Health, the New York State Heart Assembly, the New York State Association for Mental Health, the State Committee on Children and Public Welfare, and the Child Adoption Service—which operates one of the country's oldest adoption services. The Tuberculosis group has 60 local affiliates, the Heart group 57, and the Mental Health group 25. All are affiliated with the respective national associations. The Children and Public Welfare group has 15 local affiliates. The affiliates have come into being over a period of decades, and in each case owe their existence to the initial organizational activities of the State Charities Aid Association. (For the purposes of the State Charities Aid Association as set forth in its Certificate of Incorporation, and its organization in 1960, see Appendix A.) These groups are almost exclusively in upper New York State, since New York City has its own organizations for most of these purposes. In addition, the State Charities Aid Association provides the secretariat for the New York State Association of Councils and Chests, consisting of Community Welfare Councils and Community Chests.

This particular combination of state-local organizations can best be understood in terms of evolution rather than from any inherent logic. Yet because of its very complexity, the organization provides a diversity of settings in which the research consultant relationship could be explored.

In April, 1957, the executive director of the Association submitted a formal proposal to Russell Sage Foundation which requested financial support for a "Consultative Service on Community Resources and Needs." Excerpts from this proposal will indicate the way in which the consultation service that was later to be called the Social Research Service was then conceived.

An increasing number of local community leaders are asking us for assistance in (1) the analysis of local health and welfare needs; (2) the appraisal of existing facilities, and (3) the development of local long-range planning. . . .

Because the SCAA is a citizens' organization, working through local citizen groups, the purpose of this new service would be to assist these citizen groups in the gathering and analyzing of data which are essential to them in the further improvement of local and state programs in the fields of health and welfare.

The State Charities Aid Association would employ an expert in the fields of community analysis and planning. This person must have training and experience in community field research, either in health or welfare. At the outset he would have the following broad responsibilities:

1. Consultation with our statewide program groups and with our local affiliates who have requested this kind of assistance.
2. Aid in the development of project designs and preparation of suitable procedures for accurate determination of community needs which are of immediate interest and critical import.
3. Assistance in recruiting project staff for the local community studies and aid in the assembling and the analysis of data.
4. Aid in interpretation of findings of the studies.

This new technical service would be established as an integral part of the SCAA program and would require close cooperation with SCAA administrative and field staff at all stages.

Certain community organization activities prior to the initiation and during the course of any local study would be carried on by current SCAA field staff. Upon completion of the study and the development of recommendations the expert consultant would have carried out his primary responsibilities. The putting of recommendations into effect would become the responsibility of the local community with the assistance of current SCAA field staff.[1]

At the time, the writer was in Stuttgart, Germany, doing research on voluntary citizen participation in community activities in that city. A word about his background has relevance to subsequent chapters. As a sociologist, his field of special interest has been community studies. He was co-director of the Alfred University Area Study program, which for over a decade conducted a number of studies of community living in a multi-county area in upper New York State. He had been active as a board member or officer of several citizens' organizations in the general welfare field on the local and state levels. He was familiar with the organization of health and welfare services at local and state levels and with the organization and work of the State Charities Aid Association. He is the author of a guide to community self-studies, *Studying Your Community*.[2]

After being invited to direct this project, the writer was retained by the Association on a part time basis to develop plans for the initiation of the Social Research Service the following year (1958), and to offer research consultation on one or two small projects already under way. He also drew up a preliminary policy statement for the Service which included the following points:

A. The Social Research Service will offer consultation on all aspects of social research to the State Charities Aid Association, to its component statewide departments, and to individual local affiliates of these departments. The primary objective will be to

[1] Italics do not appear in the original proposal but are used here to distinguish certain statements that will be referred to later in this book.

[2] Russell Sage Foundation, New York, 1955.

assess resources and needs in health and welfare, in individual communities and on the state level, as a necessary preliminary to intelligent long-range program planning.

In some cases the director will consult with local groups to assist them in setting up fact-finding projects. In other cases, especially those relating to matters of statewide importance, he may also assume active project direction.

The Social Research Service will also function as the central source of information on all such projects being carried on by the SCAA, its departments and their local affiliates.

B. The following considerations constitute *guides in assessing priorities* and in choosing topics for study:

1. Consultation at the request of local affiliates on study projects of their own choice will vary with the nature of the individual project and the amount of time available. In each case, the request will be cleared through the appropriate department of State Charities Aid Association.

2. Other projects will presumably grow out of activity on the state level. These will be given high priority, particularly as they tie in with the network of local affiliates and have major program significance for the department involved.

3. On the state level, one or more projects of major importance and possible national significance may be developed. Such projects should preferably call upon the respective contributions of several departments of State Charities Aid Association, and bring to bear the activities of the local affiliates of these departments. They may necessitate securing extra funds from foundations or other sources, and hiring extra staff.

4. Generally speaking, the following characteristics of a project will be considered desirable in assessing its priority: (a) The extent to which it is "action-oriented," that is, designed as a preliminary step to an action program that will implement the findings. (b) The extent to which it involves on the state and/or local level more than one of the component departments of State Charities Aid. (c) The extent to which its findings show promise of applicability to the work of the local affiliates throughout the state, or have implications for program development at the state level, or show promise of national significance.

5. The Social Research Service will be geared primarily to action programs. It is recognized that in this type of project the community

organization aspects are of utmost importance, and every effort should therefore be made to tie in with local groups and encourage local initiative.

C. The following points refer to matters involving the economy of *time-distribution for the Social Research Service:*

1. Regarding time devoted to conferences and meetings: (a) the director of the Social Research Service will attend as many of the major, statewide meetings of the component departments of State Charities Aid as possible, particularly during the first year while the new service is being established and taking form. (b) It will be preferable to restrict speaking engagements on the local level to those which tie in directly with projects contemplated, being developed, or already under way locally. (c) It will be desirable to attend some national meetings.

2. In general, the Social Research Service will serve the State Charities Aid Association, its component departments and their affiliates. (a) Occasional consultation may also be given to other closely related groups, particularly those having a primary responsibility for community planning; in each case the Social Research Service will relate its effort to the appropriate component and local affiliate of the State Charities Aid Association. (b) Service to any other group will be considered only if it promotes the interests of the State Charities Aid Association or one of its departments. In this case, where appropriate, the service will be channeled through the local affiliate(s) involved.

This policy statement was mimeographed and given broad circulation throughout the various statewide affiliates and their local committees.

By the time of the formal inception of the Social Research Service, broad policy had thus been defined and consultation service was under way on a modest basis. From the outset there had been expectation that the Research Service, initiated as a three-year demonstration and financed by Russell Sage Foundation, would, if proved of value, be retained and financed by the Association at the termination of financial support by Russell Sage Foundation.

On June 24, 1960, the Board of Managers of the Association voted to incorporate the Social Research Service as a permanent part of the Association's structure and instructed its Executive Committee to develop the fiscal plans for assuming full financial responsibility for its support. Russell Sage Foundation agreed to support the SRS[1] for a fourth year, so that the SCAA could prepare for assuming its full financial support.

Projects Undertaken During the Demonstration Period

Brief descriptions of the thirty major and minor projects undertaken or given counseling services by the SRS during the three-year period of support by Russell Sage Foundation are reserved for Appendix B. But in light of the previously cited statement of what the anticipated functions of the SRS were to be, it will be interesting to review the titles, at least, of the projects encountered.

Epidemiological Study of Tuberculosis Patients

County Mental Health Surveys

Screening Device for "Multi-Problem" Families

Evaluating a Program for Multi-Problem Families

Study of Characteristics of Health Service Recipients

Study of County Health Services

Identifying Tuberculosis Patients Who Are Likely to Become Recalcitrant

Evaluating a Mental Health Rehabilitation Program

Community Study of the Aged

Respiratory Diseases Screening Study

Assessment of Need for Services for Alcoholics

Study of Parent Refusal to Give Permission for Child's Tuberculin Test

Evaluating the Effectiveness of a Hospital Outpatient Rehabilitation Facility

Study of Agency Utilization of a Social Service Exchange

Assessment of a Children's Home with a Declining Community Demand

Program Implications in a County Health Study

[1] From this point on, the initials SRS will be used frequently to denote the Social Research Service, and SCAA will be used to denote the State Charities Aid Association.

A Countywide Rehabilitation Program
A County's Hospital Needs
Emphysema Study
A County Long-Term Illness Survey
The Educational Impact of a Tuberculin Testing Program
County Health and Welfare Needs
"Youth in Custody" Studies
Adoptability Study
Statewide Adoption Survey
Multi-Problem Families
County Profiles
Social Research Conference
Christmas Seal Study
Research in College Health Education Programs

Throughout subsequent chapters, individual projects will be referred to as illustrations of the points discussed; and the success or failure of each, as measured by the explicit goals that were developed, will be discussed fully in Chapter 5.

Three other types of activity require brief mention. The first concerns publications other than those listed in connection with the described projects. A list of these publications appears in Appendix C. The second concerns papers presented at scientific or professional conferences. These are listed in Appendix D. The third consists of speeches of minor significance which nevertheless represent an activity of the SRS. A list of such speeches is given in Appendix E.

2. The Research Consultant Role

THE RESEARCH CONSULTANT who goes into an agency setting inevitably takes with him some concept of what the major part of his work will be. Beyond this, there is an undefined area which he expects will evolve with the situation. In both cases, there will be limits within which he will consider that his role is developing appropriately. He will do well to be as clear as possible both as to his expectations and to the norms he will use in assessing whether other activities are appropriate.

Likewise, the agency that engages a research consultant has some preliminary conception of his principal functions, and an undefined area of possibilities. The agency administration, too, will have more or less explicit guidelines with which it will assess the appropriateness of the consultant's activities.

Obviously, a relatively high degree of agreement is desirable between the expectations of the researcher and those of the agency. In the present instance, long acquaintance between agency and consultant, as well as a policy statement on which agreement was reached before the consultation began, was of great help. Even in this situation, however, the development of the research consultant role was a dynamic process, with repeated mutually acceptable decisions to be made as new situations arose that had not been provided for in the policy statement, or for which a norm had not developed.

In the process of developing the consultant role, three aspects are particularly important. One is the understandable difference of ideology arising from two different subcultures—that of the behavioral sciences and that of social agency practice. Another is the developing of a mutually acceptable role for the behavioral scientist; that is, fashioning a role that appeared to "fit" the situation and to have a sufficient degree of generalizability to be useful to others. The third is the development of means to cope with pressures that could deflect the consultant from his appropriate role.

Differences in Orientation

Since even researchers with social work orientation encounter obstacles in collaborating with practitioners, it may be that behavioral science researchers will experience even greater difficulty.

Relative to the problem of the nonutilization of some research findings, a committee of social work research investigators expressed the belief that the following were among the reasons their studies were not used by practitioners: Practitioners (including administrators) want easy formulas for quick action, and are not interested in furthering knowledge. They are interested only in favorable findings. They prefer dogma to research, being essentially "antiscientific." They are deficient in knowledge of research methodology. They do not wish to give research reports the careful study they require.

On the other side of the coin, practitioners held that research investigators usually ignore the questions posed by practitioners and go off on methodological tangents. Their reports contain too much technical jargon. They lack sufficient knowledge of social work practice and needs. They do not involve practitioners sufficiently in the planning and recommendation stages of the research.[1]

But the ideological gap between behavioral scientists and agency practitioners may be even wider than indicated above. The two subcultures are differently oriented in: (1) their conception of the nature of knowledge, what it means to "know" something; (2) their evaluation of the importance of the *method* by

[1] Hamovitch, Maurice B., "Utilization of Research Findings: A Report of the Research Section Committee on the Study of the Utilization of Research Findings," *N.A.S.W. News*, vol. 6, November, 1960, p. 19.

which knowledge is gained as contrasted with the *use* to which it is put; (3) the emphasis which they place on certain *values* such as objectivity, supporting of generalizations with facts, helping people, conducting "successful" projects, and so on; (4) their conception of the term "evaluation"; (5) their knowledge and empathy of each other's subculture.

This last point can be illustrated by two ways in which the agency practitioner may interpret social research. The first is negative: impatience with the rigors of scientific methodology, the feeling that "figures are cold and don't give the true picture of flesh-and-blood human beings," aversion to statistical or terminological "mumbo-jumbo." The second is positive, but also a problem: the assumption that "science gives us certain knowledge," the easy confidence that research can "give us the answer" in value conflicts, the tendency to assume that the social scientist can "solve" such practical problems as "getting people to behave as we think they should." The social scientist, meanwhile, may have equally unrealistic conceptions of the practitioner.

Such subcultural differences were apparent at times in the present demonstration. But none was insuperable, and most worked out with a minimum of difficulty. A report to Russell Sage Foundation after the first year's operation of the SRS contains an appraisal of why no problems of insurmountable magnitude arose in this merging of the two subcultures. The following paragraphs are quoted from the report:

1. The function which the writer as a social scientist would perform within this statewide voluntary citizens' association was described with considerable care and detail in the original agreement between Russell Sage Foundation and State Charities Aid Association.

2. There was a flexible attitude on both sides, seeing the project as an innovation and realizing that much would still have to be "worked out."

3. An early staff meeting of department heads of SCAA discussed and adopted a policy draft for the operation of the Social Research Service in its relation to the other departments.

4. The social scientist was institutionalized (with this term, he takes the calculated risk of inviting semantically-stimulated snickers) within SCAA at a suitable level in the organizational hierarchy: that of department head. This is important not only in catering to the notorious status-sensitivity of behavioral scientists *vis-à-vis* their (often more firmly entrenched) administrative colleagues, but for the reason that it puts the social researcher in a better position to help determine *what* shall be researched and what the relation of the research will be to the developing program of the organization.

5. The writer had enjoyed long association with the staff and familiarity with the functions of the State Charities Aid Association as a former chairman of its State Committee on Children and Public Welfare, and as a member of its Board of Managers. Although this led to role-change problems, it eased the status matter (point 4 above), and facilitated his adjustment to the new relationship.

Reciprocally, the same earlier association, aided perhaps by his authorship of *Studying Your Community*,[1] made the writer more readily acceptable from the staff's side.

6. Being on a consulting basis for a six-month period prior to the official change of positions gave the writer opportunity to anticipate and work out in advance some of the problems which would have to be solved.

Developing the Research Consultant Role

There is little literature which reports systematically the development of this type of consultant role on the state and local levels. Nonetheless, there are numerous relevant experiences that are worth brief delineation.

Two important areas contain bodies of general knowledge to which the experiences acquired in the present demonstration can be related. The first is the growing knowledge from the behavioral sciences, particularly that involving social systems, social change, role theory, subcultures, social status, and other rich concepts.

A somewhat different body of concepts is available from certain fields of professional practice. Those most relevant are the professional principles and methodologies of the behavioral science researcher, and those of the consultant in planned social change.

[1] Russell Sage Foundation, New York, 1955.

The profession of the behavioral science research investigator may appear at first glance to involve solely matters of methodology—technical guides for the conduct of research which somehow do not translate into the ongoing actualities of social interaction among flesh-and-blood people. The rigorous canons of scientific procedure, it is true, have seemed to be the antithesis of dynamic field processes, and perhaps for this reason there remains a gap between the rigorous dictates of scientific method as described in works on methodology[1] and the actual problems the investigator encounters when he goes into the field.

Such problems include whether or not he will be permitted by administrative authorities to have access to sources of data—persons or records. Also there is the problem of rapport; he must obtain real and meaningful data from informants on behavior, attitudes, and the like. The latter problems have received increasing attention in recent years, particularly in studies in the industrial setting and of introduction of new techniques in connection with technical aid programs.[2]

In the emerging field of planned social change, there is a wealth of empirical literature on what is appropriate and effective in professional practice. The profession of social work, for example, has long since developed concepts of professional practice centering around the relationship between the worker and an individual client (casework),[3] between the worker and a small group (group work),[4] and more recently, between the worker and persons and groups in a community (community organiza-

---

[1] There is a vast amount of literature on this subject, of which the following will serve as examples: Ackoff, Russell L., *The Design of Social Research*, University of Chicago Press, Chicago, 1953; Moser, C. A., *Survey Methods in Social Investigation*, Macmillan Co., New York, 1958; Parten, Mildred, *Surveys, Polls, and Samples: Practical Procedures*, Harper and Bros., New York, 1950; and Selltiz, Claire, and others, *Research Methods in Social Relations*, rev. one-vol. ed., Henry Holt and Co., New York, 1959.

[2] Many reports on social processes in field research have been published in the journal, *Human Organization*, sponsored by the Society for Applied Anthropology. A recent collection, chiefly from this journal, has appeared in book form: Adams, Richard N., and Jack J. Preiss, editors, *Human Organization Research: Field Relations and Techniques*, The Dorsey Press, Homewood, Ill., 1960.

[3] See Perlman, Helen Harris, *Social Casework: A Problem-Solving Process*, University of Chicago Press, Chicago, 1957.

[4] See Coyle, Grace L., *Group Experience and Democratic Values*, Woman's Press, New York, 1947.

tion).[1] The rich body of case reports and practice theory from these fields can be adapted to the research consultant role.

Yet professional social work practice is not used as the principal model for analyzing the research consultation process in the present report. For one thing, professional social work practice is itself in a period of transition. It is seeking to broaden its conceptual base by accommodating knowledge and empirical procedures from the behavioral sciences while still utilizing earlier subjective methods to assess results and to understand processes.

In the second place, there is a growing awareness of the close relationship of many practices conventionally thought of as social work to other practices not ordinarily so considered. The work of adult education specialists, of community development personnel at state universities and in technical assistance programs abroad, of agricultural extension workers, recreation workers, group dynamics specialists, personnel administrators, industrial consultants, psychiatrists, guidance counselors, and others has brought awareness that a new "helping profession" should embody concepts drawn from these as well as from the traditional fields of social work, and that a wider scope will bring richer opportunity for comparison and contrast. There is already considerable indication that such activities can be meaningfully analyzed within a broad, systematic framework having close relationship to behavioral science theory, particularly the theory of social systems and of planned social change.[2]

To summarize, two areas of knowledge and analytical concepts are pertinent to the research consultation to be reported:

1. Knowledge and concepts from the behavioral sciences
2. Professional practices and principles from:
   a. Social research methodology
   b. Field research regarded as a social process
   c. Consultation on planned social change

[1] See Ross, Murray G., *Community Organization:* Theory and Principles, Harper and Bros., New York, 1955.

[2] Warren, Roland L., *The Community in America.* Rand McNally and Co., Chicago, 1963, chap. 10.

The Social Research Service of the State Charities Aid Association, which became the identifying title of the project, was designed to pioneer a new role, different from any of the roles mentioned above. It was designed to provide knowledge from the behavioral sciences and research consultation as a means of affecting the organization's program. Studies carried out by, or in consultation with, the SRS, it was thought, would help to assure a sound basis for future program planning, and in some cases might even affect the basic policies of the Association. This was also anticipated in connection with research projects undertaken by the local citizens' organizations.

The development of the research consultant role within the SRS embraced four activities: (a) encouraging research, (b) consultation on specific projects, (c) interpreting scientific method and behavioral science findings, and (d) functioning as a member of the administrative team.

Encouraging Research

As its name implies, the SRS was initially conceived as a service to existing citizens' organizations, and not as a new administrative unit charged with the development of a research program. It was expected that there would be considerable call for this service, and a number of projects were contemplated at its inception. Yet there was a real question whether the utilization of the SRS on a voluntary basis would grow.

How does one "encourage" research? To begin with, the research consultant whose services are "available" to a number of organizations or to different units within an organization will likely find some individuals in positions of authority who are predisposed to the new service. Alert administrators who are looking for new program activities or questioning current solutions, may seize upon research as an activity of promise. On the other hand, many administrators and volunteer leaders may be apathetic; in addition, they may not be able to connect the little they know about social research with their own program needs. A few may even be hostile toward research, for whatever reasons.

In the case of the SRS, preliminary staff meetings considered the possibility of holding a statewide conference of the affiliated organizations to introduce the new consulting service, to indicate possible uses of the service, and in general to encourage its utilization. The idea was rejected both because of the expense involved and because it was considered unnecessary. For at this time, there were indications that there would be considerable call for the service. As a result, alternative plans were made. These included participation by the behavioral scientist at state-wide meetings of the affiliated organizations, wide distribution of a Social Research Issue of the SCAA's periodical *Viewpoint*, and wide publicizing of the existence, nature, and policy of the SRS.

Supplementing such formal means were the perhaps more important informal interchanges that took place among volunteer and professional leaders on a day-to-day basis and that inevitably produced their own definitions of the service. They encompassed stated and unstated questions of: What strings are attached to the service? Is it really free? (The SRS had its own budget, including travel expenses; thus there was never a charge for the service, and only in a minority of instances was there a charge for travel expenses.) If my organization develops some project, will control pass out of my hands? Will I be able to function adequately in this new kind of activity? Will the research possibly uncover defects or inadequacies in our own functioning? If so, are these a threat to me? Can I really trust this behavioral scientist? Or will he let me down?

Such understandable guardedness is met only in part by explicit statements, by defining and redefining roles, by interpreting and reinterpreting what research can produce, what it cannot produce, how it is done, what organizational steps may be needed in order to carry through a project, and so on.

One gets the impression that acceptance is gained not so much by methodical explanation of what is involved—although this helps—as by a generalized feeling on the part of the practitioner that he wants to go ahead with "something like this," that it is worth trying, that the ego risks are not great, that the quest for answers is exciting, that the research consultant will not let him down.

Three elements seem to be crucial in this feeling. The first is a faith that the consultant is competent in social research. The second is an impression that the consultant understands the situation the practitioner faces. The third is an empathic confidence in the personal decency of the consultant—a quality suggested by such words as "kind," "sympathetic," and so on.

The second consideration once more poses the problem of differences in orientation of practitioner and scientist. Obviously, the viewpoints differ, and when faced with the same practical research question scientist and practitioner are likely to seek different orders of answers, to place different values on methodological alternatives, and so on. Much of the resolution of this problem depends on the definition of the research function held by the researcher and by the practitioner, and, of course, the extent to which a workable degree of overlap exists so that the relationship can be maintained.

Were the behavioral scientist to be so bound up in the hardware of concepts and methodology that he saw his function only as that of "educating" the practitioner to the scientist's expertise, he could be fashioning a Procrustean bed for the practitioner and asking him to lie in it. The practitioner might do so—later to complain that the project was a tremendous bother to the operation of his agency and that while answering questions which he didn't ask, it did not provide answers that were useful to him as a practitioner. Or he might altogether decline the project as designed by the behavioral scientist, with the result that one more case is added to the long list which behavioral scientists present to each other as instances of "resistance" or "hostility" to research on the part of practitioners.

Fortunately, there are other resolutions of the problem. As one alternative, the research function may be seen not as any great advancement of knowledge or methodology, but as immediate help to the practitioner within the existing state of knowledge and techniques; as a search for practical answers required in the decisions that confront him. This may involve little that is methodologically challenging to the behavioral scientist, and little of significance to communicate to the profession. Yet it helps the practitioner obtain realistic answers and to avoid the pitfalls of many amateur "studies."

As an opposing alternative, the research function may be seen primarily as an exploration for knowledge in problematical areas of research and theory involving methodological innovations. The behavioral scientist may find such research more rewarding within his own professional frame of reference. But though the practitioner may be appreciative of such endeavor, he may assign it a low priority unless it helps him solve the day-to-day problems which his agency confronts.

There are innumerable shadings of these polar models in actual practice, but having pointed out the two, we can now identify the approach of the present demonstration as being much closer to the former than to the latter.

In this demonstration the scientist has seen his function to be primarily that of service in helping organizations confront their program problems rather than to address himself to issues of theoretical significance. This did not mean that he failed to raise theoretical questions or help to restructure problems into terms of good research practice. It did mean, though, that problems were sometimes confronted on a rather superficial level of conceptualization and methodology. These were the occasions of helping to devise a simple questionnaire for an almost routine administrative purpose, or helping a citizens' group gather elementary facts in the area of its program interest.

It was sometimes through gathering rather simple data, or through working in terms which fall far short of theoretical interest for the behavioral sciences, that a climate was developed within which a more sophisticated project became possible. This is well illustrated in the sequence of events related to the general area of multi-problem families.

At the time of the inception of the SRS, the writer was already aware that the activity of social agencies in the area of so-called hard core or multi-problem families was being carried out in almost complete detachment from relevant knowledge in the behavioral sciences. Also, it was apparent that the term involved semantic difficulties and was more an administrative category than a useful research concept.

A memorandum was prepared that attempted to lay out a possible course of action involving both certain programs and research to assess their impact. Material was gathered on whatever had been done by communities to bring agency services to bear on these families, and particularly whatever had been systematically observed either as to the characteristics of the families, or the effectiveness of types of programs.

Following these preparations, a number of community welfare council directors were invited to an informal one-day conference in March, 1959. Discussion centered on questions of definition of multi-problem families; on the projects in operation and those that might be developed, and on possible action by state and local public agencies, the State Charities Aid Association, and the State Association of Councils and Chests.

Outcomes of this conference were a convergence of interests in new approaches and their evaluation, and a recommendation that the State Charities Aid Association prepare a report on all such projects in New York State at that time—for there was evidence of the fact that many council executives, each actively engaged on the problem in one way or another, did not know of other efforts which also were under way.

The SRS agreed to prepare this document for two reasons. First, it afforded an opportunity to prepare (as Part I of the document) a conceptualization of the problem and an analysis of the implications for types of programs and for needed research. Second, the document would have wide circulation in New York, and might well both increase interest in the problem area and point to the inadequacies of existing programs.

Both hopes were realized. At a conference held in June, 1960, one council executive proposed that a carefully designed research demonstration project be undertaken on multi-problem families in connection with a Difficult-Case Committee that had been active within the Council of Community Services. Negotiations culminated in a formal application to the Social Security Administration for funds to carry out a research-demonstration based on a control-group design. The funds were obtained and a three-year project was activated on July 1, 1961.

As a result of the document, the SRS director was invited to address the State Social Welfare Conference, and used the topic "Multi-Problem Families: Some Answers and Some Questions" to point out avenues of needed research. Meanwhile, an Urban Renewal Committee in an upstate city was attempting to develop a screening instrument to identify families to be relocated whose problems would call for considerable agency attention. The SRS was called in to confer with the Multi-Problem Family Committee of the Council there, and to address a special meeting of agency professional and volunteer leaders. Thus, from a conference and document that were extremely marginal to the social research process arose an opportunity to develop research projects of a sophisticated type.

This may illustrate the point that the research consultant role discussed here consists of more than simply designing projects and carrying them out. It illustrates that it is possible to meet agency practitioners where they are, to help them move ahead with their problems, but in the process to move toward more rigorous conceptualization and sophisticated research techniques.

A related question is the extent to which the research consultant should initiate and take an active part in the community organization of research projects, against simply being on call to help with projects already conceived. Within the present demonstration, there were instances from one extreme to the other.

To the extent, however, that the project idea originates with the research consultant, there is the further problem of seeking out an appropriate group to activate the project. In the example just cited, this was overcome by offering an already interested Difficult-Case Committee the technical and financial support it needed to develop an adequate project design.

On another occasion, the Program Planning Committee of the Board of Managers of the SCAA felt in need of a statewide study to help determine its future program areas and relationship to several affiliates. Outline plans for such a study were drawn up and presented to the Committee. On the basis of these, the Committee "invited" the SRS to make the study of county health and welfare needs mentioned in Chapter 1 and described in Chapter 3.

The Youth in Custody study developed in a somewhat similar way, although here the entire study plan was suggested by the SRS. It is interesting as an example of the blurred boundaries between the role of research consultant and that of field consultant to a statewide citizens' group. The circumstances of this somewhat exceptional action are described in the report of the SRS's first year's activities to Russell Sage Foundation:

> For the writer to remain silent regarding his own ideas as to the program implications of possible research projects would have been ridiculous. Example: He knew from long years' experience in the State Committee on Children and Public Welfare that a study of the *Youth in Custody* type would:
>
> (a) Be able to utilize the services of volunteers and also put them in close touch with officials whom they should know better,
>
> (b) Fill a gap in our knowledge of the treatment of delinquents in upstate New York,
>
> (c) Form a basis for public policy recommendations in this area of program concern,
>
> (d) Form a basis for future program activities by these county citizen committees on children and public welfare, and
>
> (e) Help to improve the stature of the State Committee on Children and Public Welfare in New York State.
>
> He therefore suggested the study, and the suggestion included an outline of the way it might be carried out, what schedules and forms would be utilized, and so forth. He made this suggestion not as a behavioral scientist, but rather as a behavioral scientist with unique knowledge of the specific field of operation of one of the major operating units of State Charities Aid [as a former volunteer committee member].

In connection with encouraging research, the possibility inevitably arises that the research may in some way constitute a "threat" either to the organization or to certain individuals within it. This is particularly true of evaluative studies, of which there are two broad types. Although both have "threatening" aspects they are rather different, and it was found necessary again and again to distinguish between them.

The type of evaluation with which professional social work agency personnel are familiar consists of examining the structure and procedures of an agency in relation to accepted standards of professional practice. Standards and guidelines are provided by the appropriate national agencies. As an example, the Family Service Association of America's publication, *Self-Evaluation of a Family Service Agency:* A Guide to Procedures and Areas to Be Covered[1] examines the following areas: Constitution, By-Laws, Administration, Housing, Board of Directors, Board Committees, and Relationship to FSAA. Because its focus is on how well current procedures approximate an accepted set of standards, evaluation of this kind can be termed "process" evaluation.

A type of evaluation less familiar to health and welfare practitioners is based primarily, though not exclusively, on two related questions: Is the program reaching the people it is designed to reach? What measurable impact does it have on them? This evaluation focuses not on the quality of the program but on its results. It might be called "output" evaluation.

The writer has a strong commitment to the need of developing better methods of output evaluation of health and welfare services and for applying them widely in an effort to assess courageously the allegedly desirable results of agency efforts. Progress in this field has been slow. One reason, no doubt, has been the low regard with which behavioral scientists have viewed such research. Because it does not necessarily (or customarily) test hypotheses derived from general theories, they think of it as purely "administrative," a task for the technician.

Another reason for the neglect of output evaluation is the understandable threat it may pose. One can appreciate the reticence that is likely to greet the behavioral scientist who comes into a social agency and says, in effect: "Well, here I am, and the first thing I want to do is to make a series of studies to see if you practitioners are really doing anything effective."

[1] New York, 1960.

Whether or not good output research can be undertaken depends in part on the ability of the scientist to design research whose measures are sufficiently sensitive to record changes of small magnitude, and whose methods hold constant all relevant variables except the experimental variable. The task is not an easy one, but some progress in methodology has been made in recent years.[1] The work of the Cummings in Saskatchewan, Canada, was particularly noteworthy for its careful research design, for its attempt at major saturation of a community (so that its impact might be discerned by the measures employed), and for the candor with which the largely negative results were reported to the profession.[2]

The undertaking depends equally, however, on the willingness of health and welfare agencies to submit their programs to assessment, despite its inconvenience and the threat it may pose. Withal, a number of output evaluative studies were carried out in the course of this demonstration, including the health services study, the tuberculin testing educational study, and the research demonstration with multi-problem families.

A final observation should be added about the function of encouraging research. It was the experience of this demonstration that projects usually were initiated because of a request for specific help by a local or state agency executive (voluntary or professional), or because of a convergence of interests between agency practitioner and researcher. Over lunch, on plane trips, after a meeting, or in the office in connection with a formal visit, ideas were discussed, in a most detached fashion, characteristically with little personal commitment—purely as speculation. It was the idea that touched some special interest of the practitioner and of the research consultant that came to be discussed a second and a third time and perhaps eventually developed into a project. This being the case, the personal rapport which the

[1] See French, David G., *An Approach to Measuring Results in Social Work*, Columbia University Press, 1952; Herzog, Elizabeth, *Some Guide Lines for Evaluative Research: Assessing Psycho-social Change in Individuals*, Children's Bureau, Washington, 1959; and Polansky, Norman A., editor, *Social Work Research*, University of Chicago Press, Chicago, 1960.

[2] Cumming, Elaine, and John Cumming, *Closed Ranks:* An Experiment in Mental Health Education. Harvard University Press, Cambridge, 1957.

research consultant has with the practitioner, not only within their respective professional roles but also in informal relationships, is an important factor in project development.

The convergence of interests on worthwhile projects seems to be favored also by an attitude of relative detachment from the ideas. If both the practitioner and researcher understand there is little emotional investment in the ideas discussed, it becomes easier for the idea to be rejected (or simply not picked up) without any threat to the one who suggested it. This in turn not only encourages the expressing of ideas, but gives the other person assurance that any interest expressed in his idea is genuine. An idea that strikes mutual interest may be picked up and discussed immediately with a view toward implementation, or it may simply grow with greater interest and commitment by both parties.

An implication of this informal development of convergence of interests is the desirability for the behavioral scientist to have a clear sense of his own priorities and interests. His response to new ideas for possible projects (lightly presented) may come simply from how he reacts to them, or it may come from a carefully thought out policy of the type of project he favors in the light of what he is attempting to accomplish, what his present activities are, what best fits into a cumulative program working toward his objectives. He will not always have his way, but between the extreme alternatives of a set of projects that "add up" to a meaningful accomplishment of objectives worked out in advance, and intuitive selection guided only by general considerations of methodology, researchability, and so on, the former seems clearly more worthwhile for his professional field.

Consultation on Specific Projects

In addition to the projects enumerated in Chapter 1, there were frequent consultations of a "one-shot" or nonrecurring nature. Projects varied from major to extremely minor efforts, from those with paid staff to those carried on by volunteers or existing agency personnel. The SRS played a major part in formulating some of them, including the initial discussions of the idea and the working out of procedures. In others, it played a role in developing the research design and whatever data-gathering instruments were to be used. On occasion, the SRS assumed the principal responsibility for conducting the projects. In others, it merely served as an "outside" resource to give advice on some aspect of the design or of the data-gathering instruments, or of the analysis.

While different functions were performed in different projects, a typical relationship was that of responding to a request by an organization for help in studying a local situation pertaining to its program. The people involved were "thinking of making a study" and wanted some help.

Customary procedure was for the consultant to meet with members of the group and help them think through such questions as the following:

What do you want to find out? How is it related to your program? What use do you expect to make of the findings? Do factual data already exist that obviate the need for a new study? If not, do you really need to have the data which the study would provide in order to design a program intelligently?

Assuming that the group moves beyond this point, the following questions become relevant:

How can the questions be put in researchable form? What kind of study might provide usable answers? What kind of answers would a particular type of study design yield? How much time and energy and money would be involved in each of the alternative possibilities for a study design?

But invariably in these field situations, another set of questions faces the consultant:

What sort of relationship shall the organization have to the study? Will there be a study committee? Who will gather the data and make the analysis? At what points will the consultant help? If volunteers are to conduct the study, how shall their work be organized?

And—

Is this the proper organization to make this type of study? What possible actions are anticipated as a result of the study? If action is anticipated, is it within the control of this organization?

If not, should other organizations be involved in the planning or execution of the study? Should the people whose opinions are vital in determining whether the action takes place be involved in the study? In what relationship?

It may be thought that consideration of the last two groups of questions is not an appropriate function of the research consultant. The writer was concerned about this very point in early negotiations leading to his association with the demonstration. But the italicized sentences in the application to Russell Sage Foundation, quoted on page 15, were reassuring. They indicated that he would not have responsibility for "certain community organization activities prior to the initiation and during the course of any local study." The function was to be performed by existing field staff, along with "the putting of recommendations into effect."

Yet experience indicated that no such clear distinction could be made in practice between the role of the field service staff and that of the research consultant. There were two reasons for this. One will be discussed in the following section of this chapter. Here let it simply be said that strong pressures developed for the consultant to engage in activities he considered to be appropriate not for his function but for that of field staff personnel.

The other reason was perhaps more basic. Experience dictated that it was impractical to maintain a rigid distinction in function between research and action. For the research consultant to say, "Well, I can advise you on what data-gathering operations you will have to perform, but when it comes to how you shall organize yourselves to do it, you will have to consult your field staff person" makes about as much sense to a citizens' committee as for an electrician to insist that the hole into which he will set his fixture be cut by a carpenter. Particularly in smaller projects involving volunteer citizens, the methodology and data-gathering and analysis are so closely intertwined with the organization's ability to organize itself to get things done, that their separation becomes extremely arbitrary.

Much the same can be said for anticipating the implementation of the findings and recommendations of the study. The research consultant may have a strong conviction that he should not become involved in the recommendations to be derived from the study findings, nor in the action process through which the recommendations are to be put into effect. *If so, he would do best to stay away from the research consulting function described in this book. For by the very nature of this type of project, the outcome of subsequent action is partly, at least, determined by the social process through which the study is conducted.*

The relation of survey methodology to social process is recognized in connection with the so-called "community self-survey." The community self-survey can be characterized as a process of gathering facts about the community which meets three conditions: (1) The facts are gathered not for their own sake, but as a basis for community improvement. (2) The process brings together a broad representation of people from different segments of the community. (3) The chief impetus of the effort resides with members of the community who are acting as local citizens, rather than with professional experts, research specialists, or others from outside the community.

Like it or not, the research process, in addition to being the implementation of a particular research design, is a social process. The social process can perhaps be ignored when one is engaged simply in testing hypotheses or making surveys which do not involve the relation of a consultant to a citizens' action group. But where the survey is conducted as a basis for action, the relevance of the findings to alternative recommendations, and to implementation of the recommendations, is inescapable. Hence the roles of subject matter specialists, research consultants, and community organization workers often converge and become indistinguishable on the action level, particularly in the smaller efforts. This question will be given further attention in Chapter 3.

Interpreting Scientific Methods and Behavioral Science Findings

From the beginning it was understood that the SRS would constitute a "bridge" to the behavioral sciences, both as to knowledge and as to research methodology. As the demonstration developed, the latter came to outweigh the former, for reasons that will be considered in Chapter 5.

One way in which social science material was introduced through the research consultant was by the purchase of books for the small agency library and subscriptions to several social science journals. Otherwise, the principal means of introducing social science concepts and analytical procedures was in relation to specific questions which arose usually though not always on research.

The behavioral sciences cover a broad and varied field and include various orientations regarding appropriate functions for the individual. Those of research and teaching have long been accepted as central roles. More recently, the applied practitioner has emerged. This point is repeated here because it relates to the perception of the social scientist by agency practitioners. Shall he be considered an educational psychologist, say a school psychologist, performing a very strictly applied function of psychological testing and clinical counseling? Shall he be considered a market researcher, making specific studies in order to improve the marketing effort of the company? Should he be considered in a role similar to that in which the medical profession casts the "statistician?"

In actuality, the person who introduces a new professional subculture by "bridging" becomes personally intertwined in the minds of his co-workers with their conception of his profession. In this case, social science, for these agency practitioners, became what this particular social scientist knew and did.

The writer was aware that in situations where roles are not clearly defined, new role relationships will usually be worked out in a process of mutual adjustment in which much depends on tentative definitions at the early stages of the interaction. For this reason, he was concerned, particularly at the outset, that his role as a behavioral scientist on the agency staff be defined in an acceptable way. At the same time, he was understandably concerned about being cooperative and responding favorably, whenever possible, to requests for service. Perhaps the following example will illustrate the pitfalls of extremism, and the possibility of a *via media:*

> Prior to the establishment of the SRS, and at a time when "motivational research" was a popular topic largely because of a best-

selling book on the subject,[1] the writer was invited to speak at the state meeting of one of the SCAA's affiliates. The program chairman was of the opinion that increasing attention must be paid to behavioral science in the health education field. He had therefore welcomed the advent of the SRS and, since the idea of motivational research had impressed him as offering "an answer" to the need for emphasizing the behavioral aspects of health, he suggested that the writer talk on "How to Interest People in What They Don't Want to Know"—discussing in the speech motivational research and its importance for health educators.

The request was disquieting for several reasons. First, the writer held grave reservations as to the validity of many claims being made for the effectiveness of motivational research; second, he was apprehensive lest his audience expect a set of sure-fire techniques with which to effect certain change in the target population; third, motivational research tended to by-pass a rich field of substantive knowledge, particularly in social psychology and sociology; and fourth, the writer had ethical reservations about even linking some techniques associated with motivational research with the term "education."

On the other hand, it was precisely at this time that there loomed the question of whether the SRS would be utilized by state and local staffs not familiar with its potentials. Here, at least, was a hearty invitation by a staff executive in a key position to channel further requests, or to be disgruntled by a negative response.

In retrospect, the resolution of the problem seems simple. The writer agreed to give the talk, but stated that although he would explicitly consider motivational research, it would be only one of a number of approaches discussed, and that learning theory, small group participation in attitude change, and other pertinent materials would be covered. The staff executive agreed.

The result was that the talk offered an opportunity to relate some important concepts from the behavioral sciences to the practical problems of health education. It made it possible to show, if implicitly, the utility of theoretically related research findings, and to convey the writer's thoughts on a realistic approach to health education.

The talk was well received and apparently helped to create a favorable disposition toward behavioral science in general and

[1] Packard, Vance, *The Hidden Persuaders*. David McKay Co., New York, 1957.

the SRS in particular on the part of a large professional health staff. It avoided having to disappoint a person who had made an early service request; and more importantly, it avoided casting the behavioral scientist in the role of a medicine man with a specific set of techniques for automatic program success.

Much effort was expended during the term of the demonstration in interpreting the rationale of research methodology and the difference between knowledge "gained from experience" and knowledge gained through systematic design. A few examples are given below:

> An executive of the SCAA had been asked by a state legislator how the in-migration figures of Negroes in New York City compared with those of Detroit and Chicago. The writer, who had planned to do some work in the New York Public Library, offered to consult the 1957 special census in order to get the desired information. Particularly, the request was in respect to a pending bill which would set up a residence requirement for public assistance recipients in New York State.
>
> Since Detroit and Chicago are in states having residence requirements, their rates of Negro in-migration presumably would indicate the effect of residence requirements on in-migration, much of which —it had been alleged—was prompted by the desire to "get on relief."
>
> After thinking the matter over, however, soon after his arrival at the Library the writer telephoned the executive to suggest that the impact of a residence law would probably be so small that any conclusion based on differential rates of Negro in-migration to these cities could be utterly misleading. He did not search for the data.

Questions calling for an interpretation of the rationale of sampling are illustrated by: "How large a sample do we need for the study to be scientific?" Obviously, such an inquiry must be transformed into conceptual terms and at least an elementary understanding of sampling theory provided before an adequate answer is possible.

Another example related to sampling: "I had hoped that X County would turn up in our random sample. Why not just keep on drawing samples until X County turns up in one?"

A final example. The medical research committee of a health association discussed a proposed study of the inmates of a male maximum-security prison. It fell upon the writer to relieve a prominent physician of the notion that such a population would "be a representative cross-section of the male population."

On the other hand, there were frequent occasions when it was necessary to reassure laymen that certain data had any value at all. Particularly when studies are made on a minimal budget, as is often the case in the health and welfare field, the available secondary data are usually imperfect. The layman who is superficially familiar with some statistical pitfalls often takes an overly negative view of their use. The problem here is to help the individual see the possibilities, if there are such, of making use of what is available, but with appropriate generalizations and qualifications.

In the day-to-day communication of a research point of view, patience and clear explanations of why certain operations are necessary usually will suffice. But there is a level of greater complexity, as when questions arise as to whether it is worthwhile to "go to all that trouble and expense" to secure a certain level of validity. Here, again, the consultant may either take an adamant position, making excessive, and in many cases virtually impossible demands in the name of methodological rigor; or he may see his role of helping a "client" think through exactly what course of action he wants to take, based on a clear understanding of the alternatives and their implications.

The simple solution of insisting on not going forward with any research project unless it was adequately staffed with professionally competent personnel would have made life much simpler for the writer. Yet it was generally considered to be one of the chief challenges of the SRS demonstration that it would help voluntary groups make not *perfect*, but *better* studies than they would otherwise have made, and to help them realize the limitations as well as the potentialities of their studies for program development.

The policy followed in this matter was twofold: first, to help these groups design relatively simple projects which would bring them the greatest substantive gain with the fewest methodological difficulties; and second, to encourage constantly an understanding of the basic principles of research design and objective data-gathering and analysis so that social science usage would be broadened.

Functioning as a Member of the Administrative Team

At the time of preliminary planning for the SRS, the central staff of the SCAA consisted of an executive director, a deputy executive director, a director of the Legislative Information Bureau, a comptroller, and a director of public relations. It was clearly understood that the director of the SRS would be a part of this central group. Integrated within the SCAA were the secretariats of the State Committee on Tuberculosis and Public Health, the New York State Heart Assembly, the New York State Association for Mental Health, and the State Committee on Children and Public Welfare, with a combined total of 157 local affiliates. In addition, there was the Child Adoption Service, the SCAA's only direct service activity. The envisioned function of the SRS was to provide consultant help to any or all of these groups—on the local, county, or state level—who might wish it.

The usual method of program formulation was for the executive director and deputy executive director to confer with members of the central staff or of the affiliated organizations on an individual or small group basis, with the constituency of the group depending on the matter under discussion. But throughout the entire period, there was never a program decision involving research that was made without soliciting the writer's opinion, and with which he did not agree.

In the setting in which the SCAA found itself at the time, the research function was closely bound up with two interrelated matters that perhaps gave it a greater voice in staff decision-making than might otherwise have been the case. One had to do with the vigorous controversy being waged throughout New York State between the independent health associations and the local Community Chests and United Funds. The controversy inexorably permeated the SCAA by virtue of its close connection on the state level with several of the independent health associations, and its simultaneous connection with the New York State Association of Councils and Chests, for which its deputy executive director provided a secretariat.

As the controversy grew, a dynamic situation arose that directly bore on future development of the SRS under one or the other possible resolutions.

One alternative—and the eventual outcome—was that the central staff of the SCAA might detach itself substantially and become in effect a "house staff" of experts available for consultation and service to all agencies in the fields of its special competences. Existing staff executives provided top level resources in community welfare, public health, legislative information, accounting and fiduciary procedures, and public relations. With the addition of a research service, a varied but coordinated program of services was developed which did not have to depend, as formerly, on such close ties to the health affiliates.

These circumstances gave greater importance to the SRS director's role as a member of the administrative team than might otherwise have been the case. They also made his other roles more difficult than they might otherwise have been. For decisions about the SRS—what projects it might undertake, with what groups it might collaborate, and under whose auspices its state-level projects would be conducted—inevitably involved basic policy matters affecting the structure and function of the SCAA. It became extremely important to maintain a judicious balance in the relationships of the SRS to the two contending groups so that there would be no suspicion of having been "captured" by either. Not only must official action and behavior with respect to the controversy be impeccable; there was need, in addition, to avoid any appearance of involvement in personal cliques.

One other aspect of the behavioral scientist's role as a member of the administrative team should not be overlooked. Participation in a discussion may be closely related to one's specialized competence, or it may not be. Putting this another way, in staff discussions, one may be giving an opinion based on specialized knowledge from one's own field, or one may be giving the opinion simply of a knowledgeable person. Presumably accountants, attorneys, public relations experts, health and welfare administrators—and behavioral scientists—vary in the extent to which they can contribute meaningfully to staff discussions outside the area of their professional interests.

Status Considerations

Social scientists are noted for their preoccupation with status. On the other hand, it would be difficult to understand how sociologists, in particular, for whom the term is a basic conceptual element, could help being aware of and interested in status. In addition, of course, as they enter fields that are already occupied by well-entrenched specialists whose position has long since been established, it is perhaps understandable that they may at times feel disadvantaged. But allowing for such situations, the writer is of the firm conviction that status considerations are extremely important in a research consultant role like that being described.

From the preceding section it is apparent that the relatively high administrative level on which the SRS was introduced had much to do with its effectiveness in bringing about change within the State Charities Aid Association and with the fulfillment of its more specific program objectives. Also, it made it more important that the person selected be someone whose technical competence in research was supplemented by experience in voluntary agencies at the policy-making level and by someone generally familiar with community health and welfare services.

On the local level, the process of research consultation took place in the context of certain status considerations that bear importantly on the nature of the relationships that developed.

Among the statuses of a consultant in his relations with a local group are those of an *outsider*, a *central staff person*, a *prestige figure*, a *professional consultant*, and an *individual*.

As an outsider, his intervention in local matters may be expected to meet occasional resistance. But he may also find himself in other types of "stranger-role" circumstances, including receiving confidences that would not be exchanged among the local people themselves, or, because he is an outsider, being cast in the role of arbiter in situations involving differences of opinion.[1]

As a central staff person, he may well be cloaked in a mantle of prestige associated with the Association. Whether or not merited, some deference is accorded members of the SCAA central staff by volunteers and paid staff of upstate New York organizations. Should the individual have additional claim to fame, such as having written a book, this inevitably adds to the esteem in which he is held.[2]

As a professional consultant, the individual is viewed as someone with special competence—often exaggerated in the minds of those seeking advice and frequently diffused into areas where mistakenly the consultant's viewpoint is taken to be authoritative. This matter will be discussed later. For the present, perhaps its effect can be characterized as the expectation that he will give *answers* rather than *help*.

Finally, the consulting role is modified by the idiosyncratic personality of the individual consultant. His self-image, his need for recognition, his authoritarian or permissive demeanor, his orientation toward other people, his behavior under stress—all these contribute to the dynamics of a particular consultant relationship.

Deflections from the Consultant Role

In the preceding pages, four areas of activity have been considered appropriate to the role of research consultant: encouraging research, consultation on specific projects, interpreting scientific knowledge, and functioning as a member of the administrative team.

On the county level, the work of the SRS involved consulting with local affiliates of the State Charities Aid Association, including the Tuberculosis and Health Association and the Mental

---

[1] Georg Simmel's analysis of the stranger role is still by far the best. See Wolf, Kurt, editor and translator, *The Sociology of Georg Simmel*, The Free Press, Glencoe, Ill., 1950.

[2] Kingsley Davis has made a useful differentiation between prestige, which relates to the position one holds, and esteem, which relates to how well he is considered to perform in it. Davis, Kingsley, "A Conceptual Analysis of Stratification," *American Sociological Review*, vol. 7, June, 1942, p. 312.

Health Association. The local groups are served by central field staff workers whose relations to the groups are an undefined combination of formal and informal influence. Procedures were early developed in which the research consultant maintained close contact with the field staff worker on each local project. Often, both traveled together to a particular community. When the research consultant visited a project, whether or not the field staff worker was present, a copy of his notes usually was sent to the worker.

The consultant saw the relationship as one in which he was a technical resource, available through the field staff worker to the local community organization. The optimum relationship was considered to be that in which the field staff encouraged the utilization of the SRS, gave program supervision while a study was in process, and took an active part in following up on the implementation of the findings.

In the course of the demonstration, a clear understanding of reciprocal roles never was fully achieved with the field staff. Despite this, there was little felt animosity; rather, it was simply that role conceptions did not agree, and consequently there were continuous, if patient, adjustments. The trend over the three-year period was for the SRS to assume somewhat more responsibility for the organizational aspects of the research and follow-up than it originally desired. The result was greater autonomy for the consultant, but with diminishing systematic efforts to involve the field staff person in all aspects of the work.

Though not a major one, this development was nevertheless a departure from the optimum relationship envisaged at first, and the consultant was fully aware as he adapted to his role that he was doing so. It was accompanied by a gradual modification of what the research consultant's role should be, which seldom, however, was great enough to meet the expectations of the field staff. The consultant realized that it was fitting for him to take more initiative in relation to individual county projects than merely to act as a passive consultant on technical problems. Nevertheless, he did resist continuous pressures to engage in activities which he believed to be outside the proper scope of a research consultant, and to belong appropriately to the field staff.

The situation with regard to the field staff applied equally in the relationship to individual paid county executive secretaries. Below is a case illustration.

Before the SRS was instituted, a local county health association had organized, with the participation of several other health agencies, a survey of knowledge and attitudes about health, using an area probability sample and an extensive schedule of questions. The study was completed after consultation with behavioral scientists, and the findings tabulated and mimeographed. At this point, the SRS was requested to help assess the findings in terms of their possible program implications. While this function was considered somewhat marginal to research, the SRS was glad to comply because it was interested in seeing that the study should result in action which might encourage other studies.

The SRS therefore analyzed the findings, and pointed out areas of possible program development. An invitation followed to act as chairman at an interagency meeting in which the establishment of a county health council was to be discussed. The research consultant realized that it arose in part from considerations of:

1. A desire on the part of the local health association not to take the lead in the development of joint action, including a council, lest other agencies think that this was simply a health association project. It therefore sought an outside chairman.

2. The research consultant had worked with an interagency committee in another county in an analogous situation, and it was assumed he could perform the role.

3. Since this was an effort to extract the action implications from a study, the SRS should be expected to cooperate, even though it had not participated in conducting the study. Successful implementation of the findings could encourage competent studies elsewhere.

The interagency meeting seemed to be moderately successful, and plans were made for a subcommittee to draw up plans for a large public meeting to acquaint county people with the findings, and to develop a plan for the formulation of a county health council.

At this point, the research consultant felt that he had gone as far as he should, perhaps a little farther, in the direction of activities more appropriate to program staff, and he indicated that he would withdraw at this time.

A turnover followed in the positions of local executive secretary and district health officer, the latter of whom had been playing an encouraging role. Partly for these reasons, the subcommittee did not carry out its mission.

Some time later, the research consultant was asked that he once more help get the county people organized. He said he did not feel he could do this, and gradually the matter was dropped.

Deflective pressure of another type came from invitations to speak at meetings of local associations. This contingency had been foreseen and was explicitly excluded in the policy statement, which emphasized that the SRS would avoid speaking engagements unless they were closely tied to research projects.

On one occasion, an invitation was so presented as to indicate that the local committee had a definite research interest. This turned out not to be the case, but the SRS was by that time committed. The county happened to be embroiled in a rather delicate situation regarding the federated versus independent fund-raising conflict. The district field consultant suggested that the research consultant advise the association on how it might best conduct itself in the controversy. Because overt refusal to do so might be interpreted as hostility—since here as so often obtains in heated situations, the feeling was that "all who are not with us are against us"—the suggestion was not deliberately rejected, but rather evaded. The speech was given without reference to the controversy.

Another aspect of surveys by citizens' groups can threaten the appropriate role of a research consultant. Experience in the field of mental health will serve as an illustration.

A number of county mental health associations conducted surveys of mental health facilities with help from the SRS. Invariably, the associations viewed the survey simply as a method of gathering ammunition with which to convince the Board of Supervisors to set up a County Mental Health Board which then could receive grant-in-aid funds from the State Department of Mental Hygiene to operate a program of services. Outpatient clinics were characteristically in mind.

The SRS, however, was instituted to demonstrate the worth of using objective research methods *as a basis* for the development of sound programs, not just to document preformulated decisions.

In *Destry Rides Again* the crackerbarrel Judge instructed a jury to "go in there and give him a fair trial and come out with a verdict of guilty." Obviously, the SRS could not operate under such a mandate. The orientation toward the survey nonetheless characterized many local mental health groups and, at the outset, the field staff as well.

Usually it was possible to induce the local association to take a more tentative view of a survey's outcome and to widen its conception of the survey's value. For example, citizen associations need facts in order to speak knowledgeably in their field, and to earn the confidence of those whose behavior they seek to influence. Should they narrow too rapidly on one "answer" to the community's needs, they may be denying themselves the advantages of seeing the entire context through a detached view.

Another pressure operating on the research consultant is the expectation that he will act as an "expert"—in whatever substantive field. Should the group's interest be health care, he will be looked on as an expert on the relevant aspects of the health field; should the interest be child welfare, he will be an expert in child welfare, and so on. Obviously, a research consultant should be passably familiar with the field in which he is giving counsel. As someone has put it, he should be "bi-subculturally competent." But this does not imply that he possesses knowledge sufficient to guide organizational programs; rather, he should confine his counsel to research.

> In one instance the consultant was asked to meet with an inter-agency committee on alcoholism to advise on a survey of alcoholics in relation to social services which might be developed. The chairman introduced him as an "expert on alcoholism" and concluded the introduction by saying "We are glad to have Dr. _____ with us to tell us how to go about setting up our program for alcoholics."
>
> With proper modesty the consultant redefined his role as not being competent to give final answers in this field, but as being of help only in discussing whether or not a survey was indicated, and if so, how they might proceed.

The agency people were obviously disappointed with this approach, but nonetheless in response to questions by the consultant started to review the problem and what had been done so far. As the process moved along, the discussion became more animated as they came upon points which had not been clarified in previous thinking. Gradually, a plan evolved for making a preliminary study through professional persons and agencies that were in contact with alcoholics; for gathering data from studies made elsewhere, and for assembling other existing information about services, costs, methods of financing, possible grant-in-aid funds, and so on. As the areas of needed information emerged, subcommittees were appointed to marshall the materials and to take the organizational steps which were indicated.

The illustration sounds like a "success story." Actually, it was not, for the plans laid were never fully implemented. But it represented success at least in distinguishing the research consultant relationship from the "program expert" role, and in helping a committee face its problems realistically and work out possible courses of action.

Even within the field of research the consultant will often confront a tendency for citizens' groups to become unduly dependent upon him. They may see him not only as a consultant, but as a project director. In the mental health surveys cited above, for example, much of the secondary data was on file in the SRS office. Approximately one-half of the materials could have been compiled in an afternoon from published serial statistics of governmental and other agencies. Yet as a matter of deliberate policy, both the assembly of materials from original sources and the drafting of a report on the findings were left in the hands of the citizens' survey groups.

Also, there was often considerable pressure from citizens' groups who had made a survey to have the consultant draft the recommendations. This suggestion was usually side-stepped, even though it would have been relatively simple to prepare such a draft.

In all these instances, the decision was based on the principle that the benefits of a survey derive from more than simply gathering certain data. Personal participation and self-involvement lead to a better-informed citizens' group, one that is more highly motivated to carry recommendations over into action, and one that has gathered strength and cohesiveness in the process of making a study.

But are such outcomes centrally relevant to the research consultant's role? It is the thesis of this book that they are—that the research consultant role in relation to such groups should be much broader than that of giving technical counsel on methodological matters. We shall return to this point presently. Meanwhile, let it be noted that *if* such outcomes are to be expected from a citizen survey, the consultant's role should accommodate itself accordingly. In the process, the consultant will find he has to withstand pressures to assume responsibility and initiative which are not properly his, but which belong to citizen groups. He may otherwise find himself, through a process of "involuntary preemption," accepting responsibilities which the group itself should exercise if it is to become more cohesive in the survey process.

Conceptualization of the Role

The research consultant role has been considered from the standpoint of four types of activities: encouraging research, project consultation, interpreting scientific method and behavioral science findings, and functioning as a member of the "administrative team." In examining these activities, we have presented a number of case illustrations. They exemplify some of the field situations out of which was developed a conception of the research consultant role as it relates specifically to a social system, whether an *ad hoc* group or a formal ongoing association.

Briefly stated, *the emerging conception of the research consultant role is that of a professional person who is helping groups become more effective through the utilization of the research process.* While this statement may seem prosaic, it has implications that will now be made explicit.

Implied in the concept of facilitating group effectiveness, for example, is a clear renunciation of the behavioral scientist's right (often assumed by practitioners in the applied field) to stay within the protective borders of the purely technical consultant role (matters of research methodology, theoretical relevance of the research topic, and so on) and to blame all "social process" failures on the agency. It involves a positive helping and enabling role *vis-à-vis* the client agency in helping it utilize the research process as a growth or change process. The research consultant cannot ridicule the agency (as behavioral scientists in a more narrowly conceived applied research role sometimes do) for not "buying" research 100 per cent; or for showing resistance, hostility, or ignorance any more than the psychiatrist can afford to call his patient a cad or the physician reprimand a patient for having a bad pancreas.

It implies a positive function of helping the client understand social research; and of exploring the types of research activity that might be undertaken, with what cost in money and effort, with what order of anticipated results, and with what degree of relevance to the policy and administrative decisions which the agency must make.

It implies recognition that the agency or organization is a social system comprised of groups at different levels in varying relations to each other, and that the administrator must recognize the possible threats of the research activity as a social process on other parts of the agency.

It implies a recognition of the primary function of the agency (usually not research), and of the administrator's responsibility to his agency board, his staff, his clients, the community, to requirements laid down by national charters, and so on.

This point has been well expressed recently by a sociologist working in a large city welfare council:

> It is to be expected that the researcher related to an ongoing organization or miniature social system will have to recognize the defensive needs of the system. Operators of organizations usually know many things about their responsibilities which guide them in making wise decisions. Only a portion of the relevant considerations are amenable to research and only part of these will be encompassed within any given piece of research. Accordingly, the director of an agency is not likely to place himself and his agency in a position such that direction will shift to unknown, outside forces. Before

researchers in any social system can expect to enjoy full freedom of inquiry and publication, there must be reasonable assurance given to the leaders that the researcher is adequately informed about all aspects of the social system and that he is sympathetic with the basic values and assumptions. When the researcher does not enjoy this status he must expect the limitations imposed by the social system to protect itself from real or imagined damage. This reality is well known to persons who have engaged in applied research in industrial and military organizations. Why should the expectations be different with respect to research in social welfare organizations?[1]

From a slightly different perspective, this conception of the consultant role emphasizes that research is a social process, in which the consultant interacts with a client system inducing changes in the client organization as a social system. It maintains that the research process is a "growth process," that it will help the agency become more effective in the performance of its mission, not only through the availability of the research findings, but through the social dynamics of the agency's participation in the research process with the research consultant. In other words, it is expected that the experience will help the agency confront its related problems more effectively in the future.

In this respect, the research consultant role resembles closely a type of "change agent" role about which there is a growing literature and awareness among practitioners. This type of consultation relationship has been described as "a voluntary relationship between a professional helper (consultant) and help-needing system (client) in which the consultant is attempting to give help to the client to solve some current or potential problem, and the relationship is perceived as temporary by both parties. Also, the consultant is an outsider, i.e., is not a part of any hierarchical power system in which the client is located."[2]

According to this conception, the activities included in the change agent's role include "diagnosing the nature of the client system's problem; assessing the client system's motivations and

[1] Olds, Edward B., "Roles of the Sociologist in Social Work Research from the Viewpoint of a Welfare Planning Researcher." Paper read at Annual Meeting of Society for the Study of Social Problems, Chicago, September, 1959.

[2] Lippitt, Ronald, "Dimensions of the Consultant's Job," *Journal of Social Issues*, vol. 15, no. 2, 1959, p. 5. The entire issue is devoted to the topic "Consulting with Groups and Organizations."

capacities to change; appraising the agent's own motivations and resources; selecting appropriate change objectives; choosing an appropriate type of helping role; establishing and maintaining the helping relationship; recognizing and guiding the phases of the change process; choosing the specific techniques and modes of behavior which will be appropriate to each progressive encounter in the change relationship; and contributing to the development of the basic skills and theories of the profession."[1] This conception, however, takes its departure from the assumption that something is wrong with the "client system," whether person, small group, organization, or community. The consultant's task is to help the system study what is wrong, formulate a plan of action to correct it, and establish a new equilibrium. It is more than a research consultation relationship as such. The research helps the client system come to a clear understanding of itself as a system, so as to formulate a plan for improvement. The client system, itself, is the topic of the research.

In the present demonstration, however, the research is directed not into the nature of the client agency itself, but to the program interest of the agency. Change through the study process is thus directed to the task which the agency is trying to accomplish, or to the environment it is trying to influence.

A distinction is sometimes made between research that is oriented toward gaining knowledge (pure research) and research that uses available knowledge to obtain action (applied research). The experience of the present project is that this is not always a valid dichotomy. For the present project is an exploration of the dynamic effects of a research program on the structure and program of the agency that is conducting the research, thus sharing aspects of both activities.

It differs from the model suggested by Lippitt in two ways. Its topic of research is the environment which the organization wants to change, rather than the organization itself. And its primary orientation toward research is that of task accomplishment rather than the maintenance functions of the organization. On other points it shows great similarity to the consultation model of Lippitt.

[1] Lippitt, Ronald, Jeanne Watson, and Bruce Westley, *The Dynamics of Planned Change: A Comparative Study of Principles and Techniques*. Harcourt, Brace and Co., New York, 1958, p. 126.

Let us summarize this point by saying that the consultant role has been that of helping the agency do research on program aspects of its environment, with a mutual awareness that such research often leads to change both in adaptations of structure and function of the organization to carry out the research and implement the findings, and through implementation of the research findings in program activities. And let us add that although this often occurs where the consultant confines his role to consultation on research methodology, the consultant in this case deliberately extended his responsibility to assist the agency organize itself both to conduct the research and to implement its findings.

So conceived, the research consultant's primary role is to help the group become a more effective group *through* research activities. Within the ethical and methodological demands of the research process, he attempts to promote group growth through offering consultation on research-related matters. These include technical aspects of research methodology as well as broader matters of agency policy, agency program, and agency structure. He may do this through suggesting research topics, drafting reports, suggesting recommendations, and so on. In so doing, he assumes more responsibility for helping the agency implement recommendations that arise out of research studies, than would be the case with the ordinary methodologist, who might consider this far from his area of competence and responsibility.

Perhaps it is now plain that the research consultant as described in this report:

> Is not an administrative field consultant.
> Is not solely a consultant on research methodology.
> Is not a general consultant acting as a change agent.

The research consultant as here depicted is a professional person acting in relationship to a client organization, who attempts to promote the organization's effectiveness through the utilization of research as a method for gaining knowledge about the organization's program environment, and as a dynamic social process which will induce adaptation and change within the organization.

3. Social Research Projects as Social Action Episodes

IT SEEMS INGENUOUS to point out that a research project embraces social as well as methodological processes. Each undertaking is an episode of social action, which can be analyzed in much the same way as other social action episodes. Yet little attention has been given to the social processes in research under the sponsorship of volunteer groups.

Four Cases[1]

The following research projects illustrate the importance of the social processes. They are important in at least three ways. Social processes have a bearing on: (1) whether or not the research task can be brought to a satisfactory conclusion; (2) whether the research findings will be used as a basis for action; (3) changes that occur in the structure, function, and status of the researching organization as it carries out its task and seeks implementation.

The X County Health Survey

The SRS was invited by the New York State Health Department to collaborate in drawing a sample of a portion of an upstate county for a study of knowledge, attitudes, and behavior related to health facilities and problems. A similar study had previously been made in another upstate county. (See page 48.)

The district health officer had welcomed the study as a means of interesting the area in its health problems and of building a

---

[1] Names of counties and persons in the first three cases are fictitious but relate to actual happenings.

57

"grass roots" health organization of citizens rather than of agencies to augment the activities of the District Health Office. The existing agencies, in the estimation of the health officer, constituted vested interests and tended to preempt activities for their own purposes. He admitted, however, that the organizations had "the top brass" of the communities among their supporters.

The work involved in drawing the area probability sample was performed by public health nurses and volunteers with technical help from the consultant. Plans were made for interviewing, which would be conducted shortly thereafter.

It was apparent in the initial contact with the sponsoring council that it was a tenuous organization, and that the seven township areas under its jurisdiction did not constitute a sociological unit of any type whatsoever. Both this fact and the policy of ignoring existing voluntary citizens' groups in the field of health led the consultant to question the wisdom of the planned course of action. The health officer was emphatic about not wanting to involve the agencies. He further explained that geography isolated these seven townships from others in the county, making a wider effort dubious. He also pointed out that these seven townships earlier had provided an *ad hoc* citizen organization for a polio clinic and potential membership for a new health council.

Two months later the SRS consultant visited the project to assist in the coding of 365 of the prospective 400 schedules. A memorandum written at the time reads as follows:

> Follow-up: We discussed follow-up, including the calling of a meeting of the X County Health Council after the marginal machine runs are available. It was hoped that prior to this meeting small committees working on topics of the study would discuss the findings and report them to the open meeting of the Citizens' Council. The Citizens' Council has dwindled rapidly during the survey. Many members apparently can see no tangible benefit from the survey, but it is hoped that the interim reporting of the findings, plus recommendations for follow-up, will help rejuvenate the Citizens' Council.
>
> My assessment: I doubt that it will be possible for the extremely weak X County Citizens' Council to do an adequate job of follow-up

and action without cooperating more closely with existing health agencies. The County Health Association is willing to support a countywide effort with both time and funds, although the Council of Social Agencies is the group to conduct the survey and follow-up.

Six weeks later the consultant was in the vicinity on a different matter and talked with two public health nurses who had been active in the study. A memorandum recorded the talk:

> Mrs. Heath and Miss Yale, public health nurses, conferred about the status of the recent health survey. A report was recently given to the Council of Social Agencies. The report stimulated considerable interest, but no action. A report was also given to a meeting of the County Health Council a week ago but this was on a stormy night and only 15 people were present, including but three lay persons.
>
> They are now concerned with how they are to get action on the needs indicated by the study. The Health Council seems to be practically moribund but it will try one more meeting, hoping for fair weather.
>
> It is now realized that the County Health Council would have been wiser to call the health agencies in on the survey from the outset.
>
> It was suggested that a small group could get together to consider what is needed by way of program, and to refer needed measures to the appropriate body: District Health Office, the County Board of Supervisors, the school districts, or individual towns or villages, as well as voluntary health associations where appropriate. I agreed to read over a statistical summary of the survey findings and make such program suggestions as seem to emerge from them.

Two weeks later, the SRS sent a letter to the head public health nurse detailing the study findings for possible implementation through community action. Topics included sewage disposal, stream and river pollution, water fluoridation, lack of public knowledge of existing mental health facilities, polio immunization, chronic illness, school physical examination follow-ups, maternal and child care practices, and milk pasteurization. Copies of the letter were sent to the district health officer and to the State Health Department behavioral scientist.

However, the Council failed to generate sufficient interest to function as a viable organization, and no further action was taken in connection with the study.

The Y County Tuberculosis Control Project

The SRS was asked to counsel an *ad hoc* Tuberculosis Control Committee which had been convened by the executive secretary of the Y County Tuberculosis and Health Association. This Committee was concerned about the county's rather high tuberculosis case and death rates.

In earlier meetings, the Committee had defined three problems:

1. How to help the private physician recognize tuberculosis and to accept the public health concepts and the latest methods of cure.
2. How to motivate persons who have never had a chest x-ray to take advantage of existing casefinding programs.
3. How to convince people who had been in contact with an active case of tuberculosis of the necessity for having a chest x-ray.

As a first step, it was agreed to embark on an epidemiological study of all new cases of tuberculosis occurring during the five previous years, using data from County Health Department and County Tuberculosis Hospital records. A form was developed and pretested for procuring the largely demographic data for each case.

As the study progressed, the consultant suggested that should countywide action be envisioned, it would be desirable to have the sponsorship of a wider committee of influential citizens and professional people, and to have the approval and active participation of the County Medical Association. The chairman felt that these steps should not be taken until the study was completed and the Committee had "something definite" to report by way of study findings.

Data on 400 cases were subsequently recorded according to plan, and tables of the findings prepared for a later meeting of the Committee. It was suggested that the meeting be held in the afternoon, to be followed by the first meeting of a Citizens'

Steering Committee, in which possible future action would be discussed. Names of persons to be invited to serve on this Citizens' Steering Committee were considered and approved.

As tabulations were being readied in the office of the SRS, the consultant suggested that the Committee think about preparing a report. He drafted an interpretive text of the findings, but held that the report itself, including recommendations, should be written by the Committee. The Committee secretary indicated that she would arrange for this. However, plans for convening the Citizens' Steering Committee were not carried out, and it became apparent that if the report were to be published, it would have to be under the name of the County Tuberculosis and Health Association.

In the course of the study, certain inadequacies in the procedures for handling tuberculosis cases had become apparent. The Committee secretary and the consultant agreed that it might be better to handle these informally with the public health officials than to publish them in a study report. It was suggested that the matters be brought up formally by the secretary and discussed with the chairman and others. This was never done, nor was a report containing the matters ever presented for the approval and endorsement of the Tuberculosis and Health Association.

A number of months passed, during which the county health commissioner resigned to take a different position. In this interim period, some positive work was done in cooperation with the tuberculosis hospital director. In general, however, little follow-up was given to the initial study. A formal report never was issued; ideas for follow-up studies were not pursued; and the fundamental difficulties in the actual procedures within the county were never deliberately confronted. Yet there was some improvement in record-keeping and procedures for handling tuberculosis cases. A report was given by the tuberculosis hospital director at a state meeting which attracted favorable comment. And the position of the County Tuberculosis and Health Association had been enhanced through its relationship to the tax-supported public health effort.

From the consultant's standpoint, further work toward encouraging such studies in Y County might be possible, but was hardly justified because of the time it would take and the inability of the Tuberculosis Control Committee to function effectively as a group, or of the Tuberculosis and Health Association to follow through as an organization.

* * * *

In both of the cases presented above the studies were conducted with careful regard to methodology and sound research procedures. Withal, one failed completely to achieve implementation, and the other never reached full potential. They thus present ample illustration of the theme of the present chapter—that social research is more than simply a process of formulating and executing a research design. It is an action process, which more often than not involves the setting up of successive action systems to carry out the research undertaking, and to implement any recommendations. The latter may grow out of the former, but the system undergoes changes in structure and function as it moves from the conduct of research to acting upon its findings.

Holland and his associates have noted the process in their analysis of a health self-survey. "It is assumed that a 'self-survey' of health mobilizes the resources of a social unit—the county or community—in such a way that the ensuing action may be viewed as the operation of a unique social system or quasi-system. . . . This system operates so as to articulate, at least temporarily, the existing social structures in the social unit so that the problem of the 'self-survey' is solved. Thus, the social system that comes into being in the 'self-survey' is itself a social structure, even though temporary, which is activated and de-activated within the framework of already existing structures."[1]

Two additional cases illustrate the relation of the research effort to the social system that is activated to conduct and implement it. It will then be possible to develop a systematic analysis of the processes involved.

[1] Holland, John B., Kenneth E. Tiedke, and Paul A. Miller, "A Theoretical Model for Health Action," *Rural Sociology*, vol. 22, June, 1957, p. 150.

The Z County Mental Health Survey

The Z County Board of Supervisors requested the SRS to supervise a modest survey of mental health needs in the county. The SRS accepted, provided the local Mental Health Association would furnish the volunteers and organize the effort.

Shortly thereafter, a plan was worked out whereby an *ad hoc* Citizens' Survey Committee would be developed to sponsor the project. It would include a few persons in the Mental Health Association, the members of the Public Health Committee of the Board of Supervisors, and a number of prominent citizens representative of varied interests. Actual data-gathering would be done by a smaller work committee of professional people, many of whom had ready access to the data called for by the survey.

It was further agreed that the survey process should wait until the Citizens' Committee was convened and had reviewed the survey design.

After a lapse of more than two months, during which he had heard nothing more of the matter, the consultant telephoned to learn what had happened. He found that things were at a standstill. A change of officers in the Mental Health Association had occurred. The retiring president assumed that the new president should take action, while he assumed that his predecessor, as chairman of the Citizens' Survey Committee, was in charge of the study's organization. This misunderstanding was cleared up and the latter specifically charged with responsibility for moving ahead.

A few weeks later, the consultant was invited to attend an afternoon meeting of the professional people who would gather the data for the survey, to be followed in the evening by an organizational meeting of the Citizens' Survey Committee.

The visit was easily the most confused experience of the entire three-year demonstration period, and excerpts from the consultant's notes are quoted extensively below. The cast of principal characters is Mrs. Smith, the retired president of the Association, and Mr. Jones, the incumbent.

> When I arrived, it became apparent that:
> 1. Mr. Jones, not Mrs. Smith, had arranged for today's meetings.

2. Mrs. Smith did not have a clear idea of what the meetings were for, nor was she prepared to take leadership in organizing volunteers for the survey effort.

3. Mr. Jones, in inviting 25 citizens to serve on the Survey Committee, had not given them any idea of what their function was to be, for he did not understand this himself. No communication had passed between Mr. Jones and Mrs. Smith, with whom I had carefully gone over the functions several weeks earlier.

4. Thus Mr. Jones did not know that the Citizens' Committee was to act as a sort of Board of Directors for the survey, and would eventually be required to review the findings and draw up recommendations to the Board of Supervisors.

Eighteen persons were present at the afternoon meeting. . . . It was not feasible to assign tasks, since Mrs. Smith was not prepared to do so, and had neglected to bring with her a copy of the names of the chairmen of the Work Committee's subcommittees and of the members of the Citizens' Committee.

About 40 people were present in the evening. . . . After a brief introduction the meeting was turned over to me. I was stymied by the following considerations:

1. This meeting was supposed to be for the purpose of getting the endorsement of the Citizens' Committee for the idea of the survey, and for certain questions of policy. But no members of the Citizens' Committee were present except those who were also Mental Health Association members.

2. I felt it inadvisable to go ahead without the sanction which only the Citizens' Committee could give.

3. Nevertheless, those present were overwhelmingly already "convinced" and impatient with delay; they wanted to take definite action toward organizing the assignment of tasks that night.

4. At the outset of my talk I indicated that nothing would be done until the Citizens' Committee met, but it developed that subcommittee chairmen had already been chosen. (In the confusion of the afternoon, I had not absorbed this fact, although it had been reported to me.) One then might have gone ahead and assigned tasks, but Mrs. Smith did not have the list with her.

5. To complicate the situation further, neither Mrs. Smith nor Mr. Jones seemed to know at the start of the meeting who these people were—whether they were members of the Citizens' Committee, members of the Mental Health Association, or what. This

might be understandable, when it is kept in mind that Mr. Jones was elected President of the Association without having had previous experience with it, and then missed the following meeting. It was at that meeting that the subcommittee chairmen had been selected.

Only gradually through question and discussion did I realize that I was talking not to the Citizens' Survey Committee but principally to Mental Health Association members, many of whom were marginal. As successive waves of clarification proceeded, I modified my approach accordingly.

The indicated confusion was fairly well hidden, I trust.

Two days later, the consultant drafted a specific description of the organization and its responsibilities in the survey and sent copies to both Mrs. Smith and Mr. Jones, and to the mental health field worker. He also suggested to Mrs. Smith that perhaps she would feel better if Mrs. Brown, a nurse who had been active in earlier phases of the project, would act as chairman of the Work Committee with responsibility for administration of the survey, leaving Mrs. Smith as chairman of the Citizens' Survey Committee. She agreed to this with some feeling of relief (shared by the consultant).

With Mrs. Brown in charge of the data-gathering process, things began to move rapidly. After another unsuccessful attempt to activate the Citizens' Committee, the Reverend Mr. May, an active and capable young clergyman, assumed its chairmanship.

From the first, it was realized that it might be difficult, even under optimum volunteer leadership, to activate the Citizens' Committee as a viable unit. Should this fail, the Mental Health Association agreed to assume sponsorship of the survey. However, under the Reverend Mr. May's leadership it was possible to achieve participation from enough of the members to give the Committee some status of reality as a sponsoring group.

The data were gathered by the Work Committee; a report of the findings drafted by Mrs. Brown, and modified by the consultant. The Citizens' Survey Committee discussed its implications and a subcommittee drafted recommendations to the Board of Supervisors.

Throughout this process, the Public Health Committee of the Board of Supervisors was kept informed about the progress of the study. With its completion, the Reverend Mr. May, Mrs. Brown, and the consultant met with the Public Health Committee to discuss both the findings and the recommendations of the Citizens' Committee. A representative of the State Department of Mental Hygiene's Community Mental Health Services Division (which maintains a grant-in-aid program to help support county mental health programs) also was present. Agreement was reached to endorse the recommendations, including the proposal to set up a County Mental Health Board and charge it with developing a program.

In the ensuing meeting of the County Board of Supervisors, the consultant briefly reviewed the rationale of the survey and its history. The Reverend Mr. May, as Survey Committee Chairman, strongly presented the recommendations. After considerable discussion, the Supervisors voted, with only two dissents, to instruct the county attorney to prepare a law setting up a County Mental Health Board.

*   *   *   *

The Long-Range Planning Study

At a meeting in November, 1958, the Board of Managers of the State Charities Aid Association established a Long-Range Planning Committee. The authorizing resolution recommended that the Committee: (1) consider present and predictable health and welfare needs in New York State and how various organizations are seeking to meet these needs; (2) examine the Association's current activities, organizational structure, relationships, and resources in manpower and in funds; and (3) thus formulate a recommended long-range plan outlining major objectives that should be undertaken in the organization and functions of the Association.

This Committee was the culmination of a series of efforts to review the program of the agency, and was a small planning group within the Board to help the new executive director work out a future program. The Committee was also involved with the relationship of the SCAA to its specialized statewide affiliates in the fields of tuberculosis, heart ailments, mental health, and so on. The issue was brought into sharp focus because of the controversy between the voluntary health associations, on the one side, and the Councils and Chests, on the other, with both of which the SCAA had ties. (See page 43.)

At the time the Planning Committee was formed, the SRS was considering a study of "health and welfare needs" of counties in upstate New York.

The Long-Range Planning Committee agreed to have the study conducted in its name.

During this period the Planning Committee considered a possible future for the SCAA as a relatively independent organization structured around a central core of "expert" services, with projects and demonstrations being financed with funds on an *ad hoc* basis. Since the Social Research Service was a working illustration of this possibility, its study of health and welfare needs then under way attracted special attention from the Committee.

Preliminary findings of the study were presented to the Planning Committee in September, 1959. An indicated major need was facilities and services for the chronically ill and the aging. At its next meeting, the Committee decided to recommend to the Board of Managers that the SCAA open a major new avenue of activity in the chronic illness field. It proposed that Dr. Wilson G. Smillie, a former executive director of the SCAA and a well-known expert in the field of public health, be retained for a three-month period to confer with officials and local health organizations, voluntary and public, and to draft a specific proposal for the direction the new program might take. The Board authorized the engagement of Dr. Smillie.

Shortly thereafter, the SRS submitted its final report on the health and welfare needs study to the Planning Committee, which directed its printing for wide circulation.

Dr. Smillie developed his program plan during the ensuing months. At its June, 1960, meeting, the SCAA Board of Managers authorized the appointment of "a Committee of Board members to advise and otherwise assist in developing a program for the prevention and relief of chronic disability." It further approved "the employment of a full-time consultant on chronic disability attached to the central SCAA staff on a demonstration basis." At the same meeting, the Board of Managers requested the Executive Committee to adopt the Social Research Service as a regular SCAA service on completion of its demonstration period.

Linking expansion into the chronic disability field with the absorption of the SRS implicitly illustrates ascendancy of a new conception of the SCAA as a core of "experts" available to local communities and state bodies, rather than a secretariat for certain statewide health agencies.

* * * *

In these two cases, as in the earlier two, the research project introduced a social action episode whose development affected not only the conduct of the project, but also the course of action based on the findings, and inescapably that of the researching organization itself. The four cases, drawn from a number of contexts and representing a variety of degrees of intervention, effectiveness, and implementation are used as points of illustration in the analysis which follows.

Components of the Action Process

We are now concerned with developing a conceptual model of the research process as a social process that will accommodate not only the four examples just given, but all other instances of consultation in the SRS demonstration project. We shall state it didactically, and then analyze its components.

> A research project is a *social action episode* involving *task accomplishment* (including both the *research* and its *implementation*), in which a *consultant* enters into a relationship with a *client system*, out of which is set up a *study system*. Both of these systems undergo *planned and unplanned changes* as the tasks of research and implementation are attempted.

As *social actions*, research projects involve people who may have a variety of motivations and conceptions of what the project will accomplish, and professional subcultures in terms of which they judge the value of the research. Their behavior with respect to the project can be subsumed under the general concept "social interaction" and analyzed with concepts that have applicability to other forms of social interaction as well.

Such projects are *episodic*, rather than continuous. They are specific *ad hoc* undertakings that have a relatively clear beginning and termination. Since each is a discrete episode, each requires the setting up of a new social group, or system, to conduct the operation.

Our model states that the social action episode involves *task accomplishment*. The task is twofold, including the conducting of the *research* and its *implementation*. By definition, then, our model restricts itself to research projects that have action implications; "applied" research, as sometimes distinguished from "basic" research.

In X County the action goal was to develop a strong "grass-roots" Health Council that would utilize research findings as a basis for improved public health efforts. In Y County the action objective was improved tuberculosis control methods with the goal of reducing morbidity and mortality rates. In Z County the goal was to take such action as the Board of Supervisors would approve on the basis of the study's findings and the Citizens' Committee's recommendations. In the Long-Range Planning study the goal was to modify existing programs and develop new ones in accordance with the findings.

But it is one thing to conduct research for action purposes, and quite another to assure that the desired action will result. Two of the four cases were disappointing in their action consequences, and two were relatively successful. This was true even though all of them at the outset were quite clearly oriented toward action. Completion of the research is only half of the task, and perhaps the lesser half. Action is the greater half.

Such research projects have very little general theoretical significance. They do not add to the general body of scientific knowledge. As such, they are of little use except as they provide an adequate factual basis for action. This is not to say that they can afford to be sloppy in their methodology. If they are, their findings will not be reliable. Some of these projects can, as a matter of fact, involve rather demanding methodological problems. There is no more excuse for poor methodology in applied research than in "pure" research. This is not the issue.

The issue is that since their reason-for-being lies in their basis for action, and since the findings have little significance except locally, they are almost a complete waste of time unless they result in action—"almost" only because they may possibly involve some ancillary benefits, such as training local personnel in certain aspects of social theory or research methodology.

This being the case, the twin goals of research and ensuing implementation should be considered at all stages of the process. Thus matters related to possible implementation may influence the research design. In the Statewide Adoption Survey, action at the local level by community welfare councils and adoption committees was an explicit objective of the project. As a result, certain data from the courts were gathered locally by participating citizens even though the data were perhaps more easily available from a state legal association. The local method was employed because of the assumed deleterious effects that "Let George do it" methods of data gathering might have on eventual implementation of the findings.

Merton has made a distinction between "manifest" and "latent" functions which may be of pertinence to the twin tasks of the research project. Briefly, manifest functions are the announced functions about which people are quite explicit. Latent functions, by contrast, are functions which are fulfilled by an activity even though people may not be aware of them and even though they are not understood as the explicit purposes which the activity is designed to serve.[1]

Thus, for example, the Y County Tuberculosis Control Project performed the latent function of increasing the stature of the Tuberculosis and Health Association *vis-à-vis* other health units

[1] Merton, Robert K., *Social Theory and Social Structure*. Rev. ed. The Free Press, Glencoe, Ill., 1957, pp. 19–84.

in the county. Ordinarily such functions would not be accepted as sufficient reasons for making a study but their presence in the social processes of research projects can hardly be ignored.

Another perhaps more useful distinction can be made between the objectives of the project for the researching organization, and the objectives for the members of the organization. The manifest purpose of a project may be agreed upon explicitly by all the members of a researching organization; yet the purposes which the project will accomplish for the specific individuals may be quite different.

Taking the Z County Mental Health Survey as an example, the announced goal was to gather facts so that the Board of Supervisors could take wise action regarding mental health needs. For some supervisors, however, the survey would provide "needed ammunition," they hoped, to get the Board to set up a County Mental Health Board. For others, as one supervisor put it, it served the purpose of "getting these people [the mental health enthusiasts] off our backs for a while." The Mental Health Association, with some of the supervisors, expected the survey to supply ammunition for a Mental Health Board. But certain Association officers also saw that the survey could be conducive to greater cohesion and more interest among the group's membership, and would strengthen the Association in the eyes of key individuals in the community. The consultant viewed the project as an opportunity to conduct a survey under direct invitation from a County Board of Supervisors. And beyond a generalized desire to "serve the community," other individuals who took part in the survey doubtless had additional expectations of what their participation would gain for them as individuals. The process through which disparate parties come to agree on a particular project designed to serve an explicit goal has been aptly analyzed by Sower and his associates through use of the concept "convergence of interests."[1]

It is not a bad idea, in fact, to pose this question from time to time to the various parties to a research project: "Aside from the

[1] Sower, Christopher, and others, *Community Involvement:* The Webs of Formal and Informal Ties That Make for Action. The Free Press, Glencoe, Ill., 1957, pp. 73 ff., 223 ff., 308.

announced objectives of the project, what is he getting out of it?" There is hardly a moment during the course of a project when the question is irrelevant to the *social* aspects of the episode. It is particularly pertinent when disagreements arise.

Our model contains the term "consultant," and since the consulting role was considered extensively in the preceding chapter, one need only repeat that the research consultant here envisioned has more responsibility than simply giving technical advice on study design, methodology, and on the analysis of the findings. His consultation is based on the premise that such studies are seldom made for their own sake, and that he is attempting to help the organization's growth through undertaking research in the field of its program interests. He assumes that the social action involved in the research process will benefit the organization.

In the research project the consultant enters into a relationship with a "client system." The term is a particularly useful one developed by Lippitt and his associates in their analysis of planned change in different settings. Their use of the term to denote "the specific system—person or group—that is being helped" is deliberately chosen to accommodate all four types of clients which they considered: individual, small group, formal organization, and community.[1] In a related article, Lippitt makes a point which is applicable to most, if not all, of the research projects in which the SRS gave consultation. It applies to the relation of the consultant to the researching organization or its various subparts:

> In initial contacts it is very difficult to know whether an administrator, for example, is speaking as a representative of a small subgroup, or only for himself. The techniques of dual entry and multiple entry have developed to meet this situation. Getting into contact with the whole client is one of the most challenging skill problems for the group consultant.[2]

[1] Lippitt, Ronald, Jeanne Watson, and Bruce Westley, *The Dynamics of Planned Change: A Comparative Study of Principles and Techniques.* Harcourt, Brace and Co., New York, 1958.

[2] Lippitt, Ronald, "Dimensions of the Consultant's Job," *Journal of Social Issues,* vol. 15, no. 2, 1959, p. 10. The entire issue is devoted to the topic "Consulting with Groups and Organizations."

There are two distinct problems involved here. One is indicated by the question, Who is the client? The other is, How does one get in touch with the whole client?

In most of the research episodes involving consultation from the SRS, the initial contact was a request from a president or executive secretary of a county-level association. However, a variety of relationships were found among the memberships of the organizations. In some, not even the executive committee, let alone the general membership, knew of the project at the time of contact. In others, the projects had been openly discussed by the full membership and had achieved solid support.

Generally speaking, the question, Who is the client? could be answered by: "The client is the particular association involved." But this simple answer has complex implications. For example, if the executive secretary, president, or a small group are the only ones who know about, and are in favor of conducting, the project, presumably the consultant would do well to suggest that the matter be given broader consideration by the membership, and wait until this is done. For one thing, there may be definite, though muffled, opposition to the project. If this persists, should the project be abandoned? Or should the consultant relate himself to the "majority"? These questions are not amenable to blanket answers, nor are they insuperable. They are problems, though, of which the consultant should be aware when he raises the question, Who is the client?

But the client is not always a single organization. It is often a group of organizations, perhaps a council or federation; perhaps a number of agency representatives accustomed to working together, or perhaps a diffuse *ad hoc* group with little cohesiveness. In the SRS consultations, there were at least three types of client system: (1) the individual organization, within which the research system was either an *ad hoc* or a standing committee; (2) the combination of agencies under the predominant leadership of one agency; and (3) the combination of agencies of approximately equal status and commitment in the project.

In all three instances, prolonged consultation found the consultant involved with—at the most—three individuals in any concerted way. Usually there were also Board or membership meetings, but planning for these meetings, the tentative formulation of courses of action, was done in a smaller group. This was not entirely unintentional. The operating principles of the consultant called for acting with the informed support of as broad a segment of the client system as possible. But this is different from involving everyone in every detail of planning. It is simply a matter of what is most appropriately worked out, even if only tentatively, in a smaller group.

The relation of the consultant to the client system also involves a distinction between policy-making and execution of the study. In the Long-Range Planning Study, the policy-making body, the Planning Committee, was quite distinct from the executing body, which was principally the SRS. Policy for the study was made by the Committee and the SCAA staff, and then was carried out by the SRS with very little interchange until preliminary findings began to be available. At this point, a memorandum from the SRS to the SCAA executive director suggested possible program implications. These were developed and communicated to the Long-Range Planning Committee by the executive director.

In the Z County Mental Health Survey, on the other hand, the decision to undertake the study was made by the County Board of Supervisors. An *ad hoc* Citizens' Survey Committee was found to approve or modify the study plan and to prepare recommendations for the Board of Supervisors based on the findings. A "Work Committee," composed largely of professional people who were identified with the purposes of the study, however, was set up within this body to carry on the data-gathering process and to suggest policy-implications of the findings. But the relationship was formally that of an executive committee reporting to a policy-making body.

It is hardly a coincidence that in the other two cases, where action implementation was largely absent, the relation of the study execution groups to a policy-making body was never fully found. In the X County Health Survey, the Health Council was considered to be the policy-making body, but it never existed as a viable organization. In the Y County Tuberculosis Project, the policy-making group was clearly the *ad hoc* Tuberculosis Control Committee, but the adequacy of this group to obtain community support was never fully resolved. When the interests of the group members did not converge in a uniformly acceptable set of recommendations, there was no broader community body to resolve the differences.

In all the cases presented above there is the problem of the study group's need to establish contact with a larger group, whether formal or informal, in order to gain broad support for its recommendations and to enhance their implementation. We see that the sequence: research plan . . . execution . . . findings . . . recommendations . . . implementation is not so much a sequence of tasks, but of group interrelationships within the rubric of the study effort.

The problem of "breaking out of" the small work group to establish proper relationship to other groups in order to secure support of recommendations and their eventual implementation is largely one of "legitimation." Legitimation is usually thought of as the process through which a project is negotiated with the larger community, and through which the "community" satisfies itself that the study should be made and that the group making it is acceptable for that purpose. But since communities do not have formal structures through which to act (although their component parts, such as government, voluntary associations, businesses, school systems, and so on have such formal structures), it becomes necessary to locate on an *ad hoc* basis those people or organizations that are tacitly empowered by the community to represent its interests in such matters. Obviously, this involves different groups according to the sphere of activity that is involved, whether health, recreational, or business.

What makes this situation complex is that the individuals or organizations that are appropriate for the legitimation of the early stages of such a project may not be most appropriate for the later stages. This is particularly true of recommendations and implementation. Assent may have been attained through negotiation with the community's "representatives" for such-and-such a group to make such-and-such a study. But this in no way assures the community's assent to recommendations by the same group. Assent for recommendations may call for negotiation with a quite different group of community "representatives."

The same is true of implementation of recommendations. Assent must be negotiated not only for their implementation, but for the particular social system which has been developed to implement them.

To complicate the issue further, it is not merely a matter of selecting a particular group to perform a particular function and then turning to the community's "representatives" to legitimate it. Rather, legitimation and decision-making usually are carried out through reciprocal interaction. Personnel involved in a project often may sense the reciprocal nature of legitimation as a negotiating process. As a simple example, it may be apparent that such-and-such an influential group or person will "go along" with the proposal at a given stage provided such-and-such modifications are made in the policy-making body, the project plan, the recommendations, and so on.

Relation of Consultant to Project System

The consultant's client system might conceivably be the community, the project system, or the study system. By *community* is meant the total aggregate of people and organizations interacting within the geographical area in which the project has relevance. By *project system* is meant the formal or informal group or combinations thereof that are engaged in developing the project. By *study system* is meant the specific organization that is set up to conduct the study itself. As an example, one may think of an entire county, a particular voluntary health association, or a special project committee set up within it. Which is the client? To which group does the consultant feel responsible?

In the projects considered here, it seems most logical to regard the project system as the client system, and we shall use the term "client system" as a synonym for the project system described above. Hence, the client system is usually a single organization or an *ad hoc* grouping of representatives from a number of organizations in the form of a committee. In serving this client system, the consultant's principal concern in his relationship to the community is for legitimation. On the other hand, he is probably in closer functional interaction with the study system than with the client system or the community. But if his principal relationship is to the client system, rather than to the *ad hoc* committee actually doing the survey, certain implications follow.

Perhaps the most important is that he not be "captured" by individuals in the study system who may be advancing their own personal or organizational interests. Since he is in frequent contact with them, he is much more likely to get "their side of the story" on matters involving possible differences in points of view than that of others whose opinions have equal claim to be heard.

There is a way out of this dilemma, though it may be difficult or impossible to follow in all instances. It is for the consultant to make every effort to come into functional contact with as much of the client system as he can. He thus can be better informed of how well those with whom he is in direct contact actually represent the viewpoints of the client system he is supposed to be serving (as are they).

An obvious method for communicating with the larger client system is to attend appropriate meetings, both to hear policy decisions as they are made and to feed back information on the status of the study effort. The consultant thus gains assurance that the actions of the study system, and his actions with respect to it, are in accord with client wishes.

An additional device for assuring continuous communication with the client system is circulating copies of letters. Dictating a letter that both sender and receiver know is being received by others is in itself conducive to spelling things out in ways that assure that all parties are part of what is going on. This is particularly helpful when a record is desired of decisions made and actions taken, and also where there is need for a clear understanding of each person's commitments and responsibilities, including those of the consultant.

Our analytical model indicates that both the project system and the study system undergo change as the research and its implementation are carried out, and that this change may be unplanned as well as planned.

Not all changes that take place in the client system are deliberately planned, or are fully appreciated by the participants at the time. There was, for example, an occasion when a mental health survey in a county other than that reported here had an important impact on the SRS client, giving it a focus of activity that produced a relatively strong organization out of what had been a diffuse organization with little ability to function effectively. In another county the development of a major project led to an important change in the structural relationships between the welfare council and the United Fund. It was only gradually, in each case, that the parties involved realized the extent of the changes that occurred as an accompaniment of the research project. In contrast, the X County Health Council went through a somewhat different change as the research progressed—it went out of existence. In this case, however, the Council had never really been anything but an extremely loose organization, without a stable membership body.

Other cases described in this chapter had similarly varied histories of organizational change. This socially dynamic byproduct of research consultation became apparent early in the demonstration, and throughout its course an attempt was made to construct an analytical model for analyzing what was happening to the groups involved. Virtually without exception, a special social system had to be developed in each research episode to carry on the research and pursue its implications for changes in program. Further, it appeared that this special social system often followed a similar sequence of development, and the action outcome seemed to be related to the manner in which the research effort had been organized and carried out.

Development of the Project System

Concurrent with the present demonstration, the author was developing an analysis of the American community as a social system. It contains a model of "community action," in the sense of episodes of broadly based activity which involve local individuals and organizations in patterns of interaction not usually otherwise activated.[1] The question was considered whether the research episodes here reported do not constitute simply one type of such community action. The similarity lies in the special action systems which are necessarily involved, that the systems follow a sequence of development and that action outcomes seem to be related to the decisions and actions taken at the various stages of the development of the action system. The stages of the action system are:

1. Initial systemic environment
2. Inception of action system
3. Expansion of action system
4. Operation of expanded action system
5. Transformation of action system

To apply this analytical framework to the research episodes here described, it is necessary to make a decision as to which action system is to be analyzed. As mentioned earlier, the *project system* would seem to be the appropriate unit, rather than the *community system* or the more specific *study system*. But we will want to note that the study system develops as a subsystem within most if not all project systems.

1. Initial Systemic Environment. The initial systemic environment refers to the condition out of which the research project develops, analyzed in social systemic terms. People are organized for different purposes in sets of interrelationships that, if they display certain characteristics, can be designated as social systems. The project system arises within a context of other social systems, and its relation to these systems is of importance.

This being the case, let us be clear on our use of the term "social system." The concept has been found useful in analyzing types of social grouping, especially the small informal group and the larger, formal organizations such as factories, hospitals, and

[1] See Warren, Roland L., *The Community in America*, Rand McNally and Co., Chicago, 1963, chap. 10.

voluntary associations. More recently, the term has been applied to communities, as well. In each case, the meaning of the term is essentially the same: A social system is a structural organization of the interaction of member units that endures through time. As such a system develops, whether or not it is formally structured, some of its activity is directed to performing the *tasks* that bring its members together in interaction; other activity is directed at *maintaining the structure* through which the interaction takes place. It develops a set of norms governing the interaction of its members, and it develops ways of influencing the behavior of members toward conformity with these norms (social control). The system of interaction can be recognized as an identifiable clustering of interrelated behavior and thus distinguished from other social behavior taking place in the environment. Customarily, control is exercised as to the individuals or units that are accepted as part of the system (a function called boundary-maintenance). To persist through time, the interaction pattern must be capable of absorbing impacts from the surrounding environment and making necessary adjustments so that it remains intact as a system and performs its tasks (equilibrium-maintenance).

The systemic form that a particular research project develops occurs within an environment of already existing social systems. These include the formal organizations that are involved (usually governmental departments in the fields of health, public welfare, mental health, and related activities, and voluntary agencies in these fields), and such informal systems as cliques, friendship groups, and so on.

Important aspects of the systemic environment include the existence, characteristics, and degree of involvement of such systems in the research project; the expectations that each system may have regarding the favorable and unfavorable results of the project for its own interests; the extent to which patterns of interaction already exist as a result of earlier collaborative efforts; and the status of these systems and of particular individuals with respect to ability and willingness to procure legitimation for the project at different stages of development.

Within these systems, particularly among key individuals, a similar set of questions can be raised. For as mentioned, the interests and goals of an individual within a social system, though related to the interests and goals of the system, are not necessarily identical with it. Thus, an alert executive may be interested in a project as a means of furthering his personal professional career, while the formal system involved, the voluntary association or agency of which he is executive, may be interested on the level of its manifest functions—seeking to fulfill the community's needs in its own sphere of operations. Further, informal relationships between individuals within this systemic environment may have an effect on the position that each of these systems maintains toward the project at any stage in development. This occurs through linkage roles that give certain individuals special access to influence on the decision-making patterns.

Any new project proposal has a unique impact on each of the systems involved. Each may view it positively or negatively, with varying degrees of affect, both from the standpoint of the total systems and of key individuals within them. Each may have its degrees of interest, and of ability or inability to help or hinder the project at various stages. Each can be expected to participate in such a way as to further its own interests, and the project's interests so long as they do not conflict with them. And at any particular time, each has a potential for different behavior based on the direction current project decisions are taking.

Thus viewed, the environment out of which a project system develops is a dynamic field. Lewin has defined a *field* as "a totality of coexisting facts which are conceived as mutually interdependent."[1] In this sense, we can speak of the social environment as an *intersystemic* field within which a project develops and with which the project system interacts.

In the X County Health Survey, the intersystemic field consisted of a district health officer with strong beliefs in "grass-roots" organizations and suspicion of voluntary health associa-

[1] Lewin, Kurt, *Field Theory in Social Science:* Selected Theoretical Papers, edited by Dorwin Cartwright. Harper and Bros., New York, 1951, p. 240.

tions; several public health nurses within the Health Department who were interested in a community health effort and were available for execution of the study; a few voluntary health associations with headquarters in the county's only sizable city, only one of which had anything approaching a countywide service program; a previous episode of successful *ad hoc* action in part of the county in organizing a polio inoculation clinic; access through the State Health Department system to a behavioral scientist who could help design and supervise the study; a personal linkage between this person and the SRS director; a relationship of the SRS director, through the State Committee on Tuberculosis and Public Health, with the X County Tuberculosis Association. A feature of the initial systemic environment was that the geographic area chosen for the health survey did not correspond to any viable social system.

2. Inception of the Action System. Research episodes such as those reported here are not a part of the continuous operations of a research staff; rather they are episodic social actions, each of which necessitates the development of its own social structure which we have called the project system. Whether the idea of a research project originates with one individual, or evolves out of a committee meeting, it is usually necessary to develop a project system to implement it, and hence it is possible to identify the inception of an action system.

But as steps are taken toward developing a project system, the idea itself is likely to change. It may change to accommodate the social systems in the intersystemic field. It may undergo further changes as plans are modified to the demands of research methodology. In any case, it now is necessary to involve individuals and social systems that can move the idea along. This may simply be a process of getting one's own organization to endorse the idea and set up a special committee or study system to carry it out. More likely, several organizations will be involved in one way or another.

At least three tasks are appropriate at this stage: (1) the negotiating of legitimation from those whose early support is necessary if the plan is to be developed with reasonable hope of implementation; (2) the negotiation of an operating plan among the social systems and individuals who may eventually become part of the project system; and (3) planning for the expansion of the project system, now in its incipient stages, in order to recruit the manpower and financial resources necessary to execute the project and to follow up on recommendations.

In the X County Health Survey, the project system emerged largely as a result of the relationship established between the district health officer and the behavioral scientist from the State Health Department. These two persons, in discussions with the principal public health nurses, comprised the initial social system that put the project in motion.

In the Z County Mental Health Survey, by contrast, the inception of the project system clearly took place at the initial meeting of the SRS director with the Public Health Committee of the County Board of Supervisors. At the end of the immediately ensuing visit of the SRS director to the home of the Mental Health Association president, a project system involving the Health Committee, the Mental Health Association, and the SRS director was initiated. The actual study system consisted of the chairman of the Health Committee, the president of the Mental Health Association, and the SRS director. Both systems were to undergo changes as they expanded.

Still a different situation prevailed with the Long-Range Planning Committee, although here again the project system clearly had its inception at the formal meeting in which the study was authorized. In this instance, the smaller study system antedated the project system, for preliminary convergence of interests had occurred in staff discussion where the outlines of what was to be the project had been shaped.

3. Expansion of the Project System. For research projects to be carried out, the initial project system may find it necessary to expand. The reasons are largely reducible to two: expansion is usually required to execute the research study itself, and it is usually required to secure the legitimation of the project.

The two expansion functions, though not mutually exclusive, confront the project system with choices as to the relative weight given them. The usual procedure is to think first of the task to be performed—the execution of a study design—to the neglect of the continuous legitimation function. Seldom is sufficient thought given at this stage to the groups that may be asked to do things as a reasonable consequence of the study's findings.

Studies such as those reported here usually grow out of interest in a specific problem area field—health, housing, mental health, and so on—in which program interests of formal organizations are involved. Further, a question is implicitly formulated in the undertaking of a study. Do we need a County Mental Health Board? How shall we combat tuberculosis more effectively? What are our chief public health problems and how can we muster citizen interest in them? Such questions are typically in the minds of the members of the project system in its early stages. And usually there is at least some notion of what the answers will be—and of the implications of the answers to affected groups.

In such projects as those noted above we are thinking about achieving financial support for a hospital if the study indicates the need; or working toward a favorable vote of the Board of Supervisors; or achieving the cooperation of practitioners and social agencies regarding a new clinic if the study indicates the need for one. Obviously, a study can be undertaken and completed without anticipating the above sequels. This very often happens. But the question is: Should it?—particularly if one agrees with the assumption laid down earlier that the principal reason for these studies is not detached knowledge, but rather an understanding of the existing situation as a basis for specific action in which other community groups necessarily are implicated.

The other purpose for expanding the project system is more generally accepted: the system usually must be expanded to implement the study design. It was often at this point, for example, that the SRS was brought into many project systems.

The study system, as distinguished from the larger project system, consists of the special committee or staff set up to assemble the facts; the persons whose volunteer help is needed, to gather, tabulate, or analyze the data, to draft recommendations. Often the study system consists principally of paid staff, while the larger project system embraces volunteer leaders in policy-making roles.

Perhaps the Z County project will illustrate these relationships. The Board of Supervisors, although it formally commissioned the study, was not the whole project system. From the beginning it was recognized that the Mental Health Association was to play a role in the formulation of recommendations for action. But in addition to these two groups-in-being, another special group was created—the Citizens' Survey Committee. The Citizens' Committee was created exclusively for purposes of legitimation—not only of the right to make such a study but also for the eventual legitimation of the recommendations. This being the case, the function of proposing recommendations was deliberately assigned to this Citizens' Committee, and its members were chosen for their capacity to legitimate both the study and its recommendations.

But the original project system was also expanded through the creation of a Work Committee in the study system to execute the study design. The Work Committee consisted largely of professional people such as guidance counselors, probation workers, welfare workers, and so on, who were most helpful in data-gathering but who, by themselves, could not legitimate the project. Its relation to the Citizens' Committee was as a staff's relation to a policy-making board. The Work Committee was linked to the Citizens' Survey Committee through its chairman and several members who served on both groups. In the expansion, other members were added who were needed to carry out specific tasks.

4. *Operation of the Expanded Action System.* In most projects it is possible to identify a period during which an expanded action system that has been operating over an extended period of time has reached maximum size. This period may be designated as the operation of the expanded project system. In reviewing our four cases, we will consider not only the structure of the system at this time but others of its aspects, such as the legitimation function, the maintenance function through which the system is held together as a viable entity, and the function of task accomplish-

ment, both in terms of "making a study" and of working toward eventual implementation.

In X County this period was characterized by the use of volunteers and professional personnel in drawing the sample, conducting the interviews, and tabulating the results. More and more initiative passed into the hands of the core of health nurses who actually executed the design, and as time went on, performed a larger and larger share of the work. During this phase the X County Health Council failed to establish itself as a viable group, and persisted only through the individual participation of a handful of laymen. Thus the size of the system contracted even before the study task was completed. Meanwhile, little attempt was made to further legitimation, and none was made to involve individuals and groups whose cooperation might be helpful in implementing the findings.

As the system contracted, with only a few professionals being directly involved, it became more cohesive, and more time could be taken from system-maintenance activities and transferred to task accomplishment. Thus a good study was produced by what ended as a small cohesive group, although this was not the group that could effect the broad implementation desired. The consultant's relationship was chiefly with the district health officer and the director of public health nurses. It was impossible to establish a working relationship with a larger "client system," because the attempt to create such a system out of a number of diffusely interested individuals was ineffective.

The Y County Tuberculosis Control Committee underwent only a minimal expansion for the project, and this expansion was exclusively for task accomplishment purposes related to the study itself. At its high point, it involved the original committee and two professional research consultants, a part-time person to assist in data processing, and some nursing and clerical personnel to obtain the desired data from the records at the Health Office and the Tuberculosis Hospital. Expansion for continued legitimation and for the implementation phase of the project, particularly as this entailed the cooperation of practicing physicians, never was carried out. Some incidental implementation developed as data on tuberculosis control that emerged from the study process were fed back into the Health Department and the Tuberculosis Hospital. The adjustments were minimal, however, when compared with the potential for change which the study uncovered.

In contrast to the X County Health Council, the *ad hoc* Tuberculosis Control Committee was a clearly distinct and formally organized unit, whose planning meetings were usually well attended. The minutes of these meetings indicated a strong group that was making definite progress, but between meetings it is questionable whether the patterned interaction, the boundaries, and the task performance were strong enough to characterize the Committee as a social system. The tasks of gathering and processing the data were performed by individuals; the Committee in effect did not exist between meetings. Some minimal changes occurred as a result. The system never became strong enough to utilize fully what had been found, to modify existing procedures, to develop new programs, or to plan more specific action-oriented studies, as had initially been intended.

At its fully expanded stage, the Z County project system consisted of a number of components whose relation to each other was fairly clearly defined. The Health Committee of the Board of Supervisors, the Citizens' Survey Committee, the Work Committee, and the consultant were interrelated in a cohesive way at this stage, despite the difficulty with the organization of the Citizens' Survey Committee. At the periphery of this nucleus were the Board of Supervisors and the Mental Health Association. Legitimation was given definite attention throughout the course of the study, and the action system's expansion was not only for task performance in terms of making a study (the specific function of the Work Committee) but to provide for eventual implementation. This latter was accomplished by expanding the system to include individuals in the Citizens' Committee who could legitimate the recommendations and their implementation.

The Long-Range Planning Study represented a rather different situation during this operational phase of the expanded action system. In this case, an action system already existed in the form of a Board Committee and a staff that could help it. Here was a Board Committee that needed facts, here was a staff whose usual function was to be of service to such a Board Committee. Thus the development of a project to study health and welfare needs in upstate New York was a routine operation in terms of structure and function. It differs from the other cases in this respect; yet the difference is only of degree. For inevitably a special subsystem arose around the project involving the consultant, the executive director, the deputy executive director, the Committee chairman, and the president of the SCAA, even though staff expansion and *ad hoc* legitimating body were not required to produce recommendations to the Board of Managers. This is the only case in which the relation of the consultant to the project system was clearly defined before the project began. The consultant was a component of the client organization, rather than part of a separate *ad hoc* project system.

5. *Transformation of the Action System.* As action episodes, the projects under consideration have identifiable beginnings in which an action system emerges. The system is then expanded to legitimate the study, to execute it, and to anticipate the implementation of the study findings. A final stage can be identified which may be called the "transformation of the action system."

Often it is only at this point that thought is given to the social processes that are necessary if implementation is to be achieved. Since the social system that can implement the recommendation is usually not the social system that conducts the study, a discontinuity—often a break—can occur unless action is taken in the earlier stages toward developing an implementing system. The cohesiveness of the *ad hoc* project system up to this point has been increased by a common effort to perform a task—to make a study. But as the study aspect draws to a close, has the project system acquired the legitimating and implementing strength to carry the recommendations into action?

There are several "fates" of the action system that may be desired: (a) the special project system may establish itself as a permanent organization with a program that includes implementation of the study findings; (b) the project system may be seen merely as a means to a study and its implementation, with the idea that the system will dissolve when its mission is accomplished; (c) the project system may work toward the establishment of another action system, after which it will dissolve; (d) the project system may have antedated the project, and may continue to exist in essentially the same form after the project is terminated. Each of these possibilities is illustrated by one of our cases: (a) although the X County Health Survey did not succeed in its dual purpose of developing a strong council that would in turn implement the findings, this was the clear intent; (b) the Y County Tuberculosis Committee saw itself as an *ad hoc* committee with an *ad hoc* purpose; (c) the Z County Mental Health Survey was similarly set up as a temporary, *ad hoc* venture, with the general knowledge that the major outcome would be the decision to establish, or not to establish, a county Mental Health Board—no permanence was envisaged for the project system itself; (d) the Long-Range Planning Committee's assignment of a study task to the SRS was an action episode clearly within the established ongoing organizational structure.

Aside from these specific outcomes, however, other changes may take place among the social systems engaged in such a project. These changes may be anticipated or unexpected, hoped for or unwelcome. Thus the Long-Range Planning Committee, which had initially seen the survey of health and welfare needs as only an incident in its total mission, utilized the study as the basis for its ultimate recommendations and then negotiated its own dissolution. The Committee was certainly not set up for the purpose of making this particular study, or of limiting its recommendations to the study's findings. (See page 66.) Apparently, there was a feeling that the development of the new chronic illness program would constitute a major drain on staff and Board time, thus making other areas of planning and program development academic. No doubt it also was aware of the gradual transformation, in part hastened by the study, of the concept of the SCAA's principal function from that of a service organization for its historical affiliates to a central core of expert services. A major, more or less unanticipated consequence of the study, then, was the enactment of the new structure and function of the

SCAA. The presence of the SRS constituted a sort of "test-run" of how the new SCAA would look and operate.

It is interesting to relate this experience to part of the rationale for mental health consultation developed by Caplan and his associates in the Harvard School of Public Health. Caplan points out that the individual in a crisis may seek to resolve it in ways that may establish a new pattern within the social system of which he is a part. "The significance of a crisis is in the temporal telescoping of development which it manifests. Major alterations in pattern may occur in a relatively short period of time, and may subsequently remain stable for a long time to come."[1]

The analogy of the group research project to individual crisis is fitting in two ways. First, the idea for a research project may have arisen out of a crisis. For example, the organization may be in a crisis of apathy and diffuseness, and "doing a study" is seen as a way of attaining cohesiveness and common purpose. This was true of some of the mental health studies, and, in a sense, of the X County Health Survey. Secondly, the development of a study, often involving a new social system with possibly unanticipated effects on existing systems through its recommendations and their implementation, may itself constitute a crisis situation out of which the organization emerges in an altered pattern which then persists over a considerable period of time. Thus it would seem important for the professional research consultant to be aware of the process, and to take more responsibility for the dynamic aspects of his own behavior than he usually does.

A final point about the research process as a social action episode can be introduced by quoting a colleague concerning the type of analysis here developed: "I don't believe you should call a research project an action episode unless it leads to action. All too frequently such projects do not; and sometimes they are even used as a means of *avoiding* action."

---

[1] Caplan, Gerald, "A Conceptual Framework for Preventive Psychiatry" in Lindemann, Erich, and Gerald Caplan, *Explorations in Preventive Psychiatry*. Basic Books, New York. In preparation.

The difficulty here is purely verbal. People usually have implementation in mind when they think of "action." Although a study is an action episode, its findings may not themselves become implemented in action. Often, they are not. But lack of implementation does not preclude that the study process itself is an action episode, and often a highly consequential one, as indicated. If implementation does not result, then this is an independent matter and should be so analyzed. It is hoped that the framework developed in this chapter may be useful in the process.

4. Goal Setting and Goal Displacement

IN APPRAISING THE DEGREE OF SUCCESS of any venture, two questions are relevant: Were the goals that were sought worthwhile? To what extent were they attained? Obviously, neither question can be answered unless the goals involved are specified. Yet it is precisely at this point that many ventures in the health and welfare field are ambiguous. They specify a number of activities whose value may be tacit or explicitly claimed, and then assess success or failure according to the extent to which these activities have been carried on substantially as described. This yields evaluational material of approximately this order: We set out to do so-and-so, and we were actually able to do it to such-and-such an extent. Even this rather minimal level of evaluation is often not carried through in any systematic way.

Goal Setting

Behind the question of the extent to which the purported activities in a project actually were carried out there lies a more difficult question: To what extent did the activities further the purposes it was assumed they would further? As we shall see, this question is easier to raise than to answer.

One reason this more difficult type of evaluation seldom is made is that it may never occur to those involved to determine systematically why such activities are assumed to be desirable.

If this is considered to be an indictment of current social service practice, then that indictment must include the Social Research Service demonstration project. For although the project in many respects had the advantage of excellent preliminary planning, it was launched and well under way before it was decided to spell out not only the activities whose performance was aspired to, but also the purposes which these activities presumably would serve.

In this chapter and the next we shall be concerned with the general question of the extent to which the SRS project was "successful." We shall use as our analytical framework four concepts: goal setting, goal displacement, goal attainment, and goal failure (or nonattainment). Under goal setting, we shall examine not only the goals that gradually evolved during the first year of the demonstration, but the processes through which goals became set for the individual project episodes and for the SRS project itself.

Frequently, a number of conflicting goals compete for consideration in the decision-making and action process, so that while an activity's announced goals may be A, B, and C, it may find itself operating to further goals X, Y, and Z. This is called "goal displacement," and we shall find the concept helpful in subjecting the SRS demonstration to scrutiny for evidences of the process—which, let the reader be warned, will be many. In the next chapter, we shall analyze some types of goal attainment and goal failure, looking for whatever generalizations the data seem to warrant.

The Social Research Service Project Goals

The basic function of the SRS was phrased in one passage from the original request to Russell Sage Foundation for financial support as follows:

> Because the SCAA is a citizens' organization, working through local citizen groups, the purpose of this new service would be to assist these citizen groups in the gathering and analyzing of data which are essential to them in the further improvement of local and state programs in the fields of health and welfare.

The initial policy statement of the SRS contained a similar passage:

> The primary objective will be to assess resources and needs in health and welfare in individual communities and on the statewide

level as a necessary preliminary to intelligent long-range program planning.

The purpose described in these statements was supplemented, at least tacitly, by an additional initial purpose: To provide knowledge and concepts from the behavioral sciences to practitioners that may be of use in analyzing their experiences in the community.

During the first year's operation, as the writer was considering how the experience might eventually be reported and evaluated, it became apparent that the objectives here posed were not sufficiently specific to distinguish other vaguely enunciated goals that seemed to be involved. He therefore formulated them more explicitly in the outline given below, which will be used as a basis for assessment in this and the following chapters.

The first four of these goals were seen as related to the client's organization, deriving from the demonstration's purpose of promoting organizational effectiveness through the behavioral research activities. The formulation read:

> To promote the client organization's growth in effectiveness through:
> 1. Encouraging careful research for program planning and operation. This involves help in conducting specific studies and also help in imparting attitudes and techniques for critical evaluation.
> 2. Encouraging action in implementing the studies involved. This includes both program modifications and innovations as a result of the study findings, and changes in organizational structure or behavior as a result of the research episode.
> 3. Helping client organizations acquire a greater awareness of the behavioral components of their work.
> 4. Helping client organizations improve their general position in the community.

Three additional goals were concerned not so much with the client organization, but with the utilization of behavioral science techniques in health and welfare organizations and agencies. They thus had wider applicability, if lower priority, than the first four:

5. Devising tools, methods, and procedures which might be useful elsewhere in New York State and other parts of the country.

6. Obtaining study findings which would have program implications elsewhere in New York State and other parts of the country.

7. Encouraging utilization of research in health and welfare organizations and agencies of various types throughout New York State and in other parts of the country.

These, then, are the goals that were set for the activities of the Social Research Service, and against which the impact of its activities will be assessed. They were formulated not by negotiation of the principal parties, or even in advance of the project. Rather, they were developed by the writer principally in anticipation of making the present summary evaluation. Had this document not been in the offing, it is questionable whether they ever would have been made explicit. With this acknowledgment, the writer can be free of self-congratulation in pointing out the widespread lack of goal clarification in many other demonstration projects.

It perhaps also should be noted that the goals were formulated over a period of time. They evolved out of the process of trying to make a "fit" between what was being done, or was being aspired to, and what seemed to be the motivation for it. And, as we shall shortly see, this progressive and intermittent characteristic also applied to goal displacement, goal success, and goal failure.

At the project level, the initial SRS policy statement (see Chapter 1) served as a guide in the decisions whether or not to become engaged in specific efforts. There was no feeling, however, that the policy must be followed slavishly. In fact, certain departures were deliberately taken, particularly as relations between the SCAA and its statewide affiliates became less intertwined. With this development, for instance, more autonomy was assumed by the SRS in making direct contact with local groups rather than always using the affiliate as an intermediary. Thus the policy statement served to describe an "ideal type" of relationship. Where it did not fit the activities which were developing, the prescribed relationships, themselves, were just as readily changed to conform to the activities as the reverse.

Why should one change "policy" to conform to practice? It would seem folly not to do so if the practice seems more in keeping with what is really desired than is the policy. It was precisely at this point that clear enunciation of the project goals seemed necessary, and it was this set of circumstances which resulted in goal setting for the total project becoming a progressive and continuing process.[1]

The process of goal setting at the project level was extremely varied, but some observations can be made about it. Generally speaking, the initial encounter of the consultant with the client system was devoted to this process. At most of these exploratory meetings the consulting relationship between the SRS and the group was very much in the forefront of the discussions. Less apparent, perhaps, but also taking place, was a convergence of interests.

The consultant was trying to determine whether this group and situation "fitted" his conception of one in which he could be useful in connection with the policy and goals of the SRS. At the same time, the client group was obtaining an assessment of what it might reasonably expect from the SRS. Often this involved an initial disappointment on the part of the client group, as it found that a dependency relationship to the consultant was being resisted, and that he was either unwilling or unable to "give them the answers," or "tell them what they ought to do." If out of this reciprocal testing there emerged a convergence of interests, the relationship was reinforced and continued. If not, it was dropped at this point.

Meanwhile, there was a reciprocal process of goal exploration and clarification as the consultant inquired into what the client group had in view, what sort of research it was considering, what resources it could dispose for the research, what kinds of data

---

[1] Perhaps one should note the close affinity between what is described here and John Dewey's basic approach to ethical values as a growing and developing process, rather than a set of dicta possessing *a priori* validity. The reciprocal testing of values and experience as a continuous process is also basic to the work of Mary P. Follett, notably her *Creative Experience*, Longmans Green and Co., New York, 1924.

might be expected, how useful such data would be to the group, and so forth.

Usually there emerged from the exploratory session a rather clear decision either to go ahead with a research project or to drop it. Where a consulting relationship to a project was actually developing, the meeting often resulted in a fairly definite preliminary agreement as to the nature of the project, its approximate magnitude in terms of manpower and money, the extent to which the consultant would be of help, and the general organizational plans for the project system.

In retrospect, it seems rather remarkable to accomplish all that indicated above in what usually was a session lasting no more than two to three hours. But again, little was settled once and for all on such occasions, even though the broad outlines were explored and roughly agreed upon.

Further, there was seldom or never a formally drawn up "agreement" defining the relationship, its mutual responsibilities, and goals, or the specific methodology to be employed. These were often accomplished through follow-up letters, minutes of meetings, and the formulation of study protocols. In some instances, study designs were developed which specified purposes, related the undertaking to other efforts and to the literature, spelled out the methodology, and so on. But there was no systematic provision for this, and often, as will be seen in the following chapter, a price was paid for such casual procedure.

Withal, one conclusion has emerged clearly from the SRS experience: early and systematic provision should be made for the preparation of documents prescribing the mutual responsibilities in the relationship, the purposes of the project, its methodology, and the structure of the project system. Also, plans for implementation should be drawn up as soon as feasible. Even in the matter of publication of the study findings, or of further analyses of the data, a clear understanding may avoid later disagreements over confidentiality and publishing rights.

None of these decisions need be considered irrevocable or immune to renegotiation. But the formal recording of such preliminary decisions will help to clarify goals, avoid misunder-

standings, and in other ways assist the project to an action outcome. As the project develops, practice may reveal a divergence
between what is occurring and what was proposed. This can
provide occasion to readjust practice to established procedures,
or to renegotiate earlier procedures in the light of subsequent
experience.

In the preceding chapter, an excellent example of misunder-
standings caused by haziness is afforded by the Y County Tuberculosis Project. The study findings of the epidemiology of active
cases showed the usual picture of high incidence among males,
particularly in the older age groups, of concentration of cases in
low-income neighborhoods, and so on. But as the results became
available, it was apparent that the health commissioner had
hoped that the study would somehow yield much more dramatic
data which he could take to the county's physicians to goad them
into more effective individual case diagnosis and control. He
therefore demurred from soliciting the support of the physicians
for a countywide effort "until we really have something to tell
them." It was thus impossible to engage them in legitimating the
implementation of the findings. He also lost interest in moving on
from the original plan of using the epidemiological study only as a
preliminary to other, more pointed types of project.

Perhaps the most obvious example of the importance both of
goal setting and earlier redefinition of goals was in the series of
county mental health surveys, of which the Z County Mental
Health Survey was one. As detailed in Chapter 3, the Z County
procedure was atypical, in that a thorough effort was made to
spell out relationships, purposes, mutual responsibilities in writing, and to communicate with all principal parties through
follow-up letters. Ironically, it was in this project that the most
complete misunderstanding of relationships during the initial
stages occurred. But the purposes of the study were carefully
worked out, and the relation of the findings to follow-up action
was clearly thought through from the outset, both of which
appear to have a bearing on the eventual favorable outcome.

Yet clear goal setting and the spelling out of reciprocal obligations do not of themselves automatically ensure success—as the

mental health surveys illustrate in another way. The consultant was deliberately specific that as a condition of the consulting relationship the SRS would be given the opportunity to review the draft of any report before it was publicized. No veto or censoring power was involved; it was done only as a service in a technically difficult field, and because the reputation of the SRS was associated with the projects. Despite the clearest agreement on this prerogative, two of the reports were published without the SRS having the opportunity to review the preliminary draft.

On balance, nonetheless, agreements have been helpful, and confusion over respective responsibilities would probably have been more frequent had not these matters been spelled out to the extent that they were.

Goal Displacement

Social structures that have been established to achieve certain goals often behave in a way that seems remote from their original purpose. For example, a religion of simplicity becomes institutionalized with a complex priestly hierarchy and a rich symbolism. A revolutionary movement in the name of individual rights becomes congealed into a government that usurps those rights. The labor union that is to serve its members becomes their master. In short, the implementation of a purpose through a social system often involves activities by that social system that are not conducive to fulfilling its original purpose.

This phenomenon, widely recognized over the centuries, has in the past few decades been analyzed especially as it relates to those formal, rationalized, impersonal hierarchical administrative systems called bureaucracies. The process has been called "goal displacement." In his essay on "Bureaucratic Structure and Personality," Merton observes that a strong organizational discipline is needed for a system to perform its announced functions in a reliable fashion. The discipline must be supported by sentiment on the part of the officials, which often grows stronger than is necessary. "But this very emphasis leads to a transference of the sentiments from the *aims* of the organization onto the particular details of behavior required by the rules. Adherence to the rules, originally conceived as a means, becomes transformed into an end-in-itself; there occurs the familiar process of *displacement* of goals whereby 'an instrumental value becomes a terminal value.' "[1]

Selznick has formulated the process as follows:

> Running an organization, as a specialized and essential activity, generates problems which have no necessary (and often an opposed) relationship to the professed or "original" goals of the organization. The day-to-day behavior of the group becomes centered around specific problems and proximate goals which have primarily an internal relevance. Then, since these activities come to consume an increasing proportion of the time and thoughts of the participants, they are—from the point of view of actual behavior—*substituted* for the professed goals.[2]

Goal Displacement in the Social Research Service Projects

In the research episodes reported here, as well as in the SRS demonstration as a whole, there were evidences of goal displacement behavior. In analyzing them, our concern will not be with the specific weals or woes of the SRS project so much as with the types of goal displacement activity that may be encountered in other research episodes as well.

In Chapter 3 we emphasized that one characteristic of research episodes is that they require the establishment of a separate *ad hoc* action system. As separate systems, these project systems are hardly prime examples of typical bureaucratic structures. Rather, part of their peculiar challenge and interest is that they are new creations, involving nonroutinized procedures, without a "rule book," and lacking most of the classical characteristics of bureaucratic structure outlined by Max Weber.[3] Indeed, much of the preceding section indicates that had the relationships been more deliberately formalized in some of these projects, certain difficulties might have been avoided.

[1] Merton, Robert K., *Social Theory and Social Structure*. Rev. ed. The Free Press, Glencoe, Ill., 1957, p. 199.

[2] Selznick, Philip, "An Approach to a Theory of Bureaucracy," *American Sociological Review*, vol. 8, February, 1943, p. 48.

[3] See Chapter 8, Bureaucracy, in Gerth, H. H., and C. Wright Mills, editors, *From Max Weber:* Essays in Sociology, Oxford University Press, New York, 1946.

Nevertheless, the organizations represented in the project system themselves often embodied many of the characteristics of bureaucratic structure; and the special *ad hoc* project system in some cases generated enough coherence, sentiment, and stability to experience goal displacement in its own right. The same applies to the SRS. As it established itself as an integral part of the permanent administrative structure of the SCAA, the SRS became subject to the very types of organizational pressures from which goal displacement results. As with other organizations, it came to be a force in its own right, acting not only toward performing its declared functions but also toward maintaining itself as a viable entity.

There is one source of counter-pressure that to some extent immunizes the consultant from pressures toward goal displacement by the administrative system's interests. This is the possibility that he may have a stronger tie to his profession than to the organization in which he finds himself. Gouldner points out that the technical expert's administrative superior may be unqualified to judge him, and that he must ultimately be judged from outside the administrative organization. He continues:

> This, in turn, means that the technical expert himself is often dependent on persons outside his organization to validate his position within it. Consequently, his work must manifest a high degree of concern for the maintenance of technical standards. This not only disposes the expert to resist imperative pressures for "results," coming from his superiors, but it also makes him less vulnerable to control from those within and in command of his organization.[1]

The consultant as a "technical expert" may thus be less sensitive than line executives to the administrative demands of the organization, whether these be in the direction of the organization's professed goals, or a set of substituted goals. Indeed, as mentioned in Chapter 3, the tug of the professional reference group may be so great that he is unable to confront adequately the responsibilities he has incurred to the organization.

[1] Gouldner, Alvin W., "Organizational Analysis" in Merton, Robert K., Leonard Broom, and Leonard S. Cottrell, Jr., editors, *Sociology Today:* Problems and Prospects. Basic Books, New York, 1959, p. 415.

Goal displacement pressures can be expected from at least three directions. The first is the tendency for the research staff, like other groups in a bureaucratic organization, toward growth in numbers, budget, space, and "status"—the familiar phenomenon of "empire-building." The crucial differentia here is whether the expansion is rationally related to the increased performance of relevant goal-attainment behavior. So long as this expansion serves the announced goals, rather than usurping them, and so long as the announced goals are subordinated to the organization's overall goals, expansion can take place without such goal displacement.

The second source of goal displacement may come from the surrounding bureaucratic structure. This is the pressure to look for "quick results" at the expense of validity. This pressure may come from the executive or practitioner staff, particularly in situations where their own performance is judged more on the basis of symbols of accomplishment than on more substantial but less dramatic attainments. To the extent that the research consultant identifies himself with the organization, he is susceptible to this type of pressure.

The third type of pressure toward goal displacement comes from the consultant's professional identification outside the organization. He may confront situations in which the objectives of his profession appear more congenial than the organizational objectives he purportedly is furthering. In reality, these objectives are seldom directly opposed. (Indeed, if they are too dissident, one might question either the wisdom or the integrity of the consultant: one usually avoids entering into conflicting sets of commitments that cannot be compatibly discharged.) Rather, it is a question of the priority of relevant values in the subcultures of practitioner and scientist. (See page 21.) Should the scientist favor his values at the sacrifice of those of his organization, he is likely to find that somehow he is "misunderstood," or, "they really don't want research, they simply want the trappings of research," and so on. Agreement on commonly acceptable goals is, however, essential. In the absence of specification and acceptance, goal displacement may be discussed in general, but without resolution, since one man's goal attainment becomes another man's goal displacement.

In considering goal displacement, we shall use the specific goal statement of the SRS. Obviously, this is not the only possible set of goals for a research staff, and no ultimate claims are made for it. We shall not examine the validity of the goals; only the extent to which the SRS departed from behavior that could reasonably be expected to achieve them. To the extent, then, that other research staffs in analogous situations pursue the same goals with the same priority, they may expect to experience many of the pressures toward goal displacement which the SRS experienced.

In generalizing from the SRS experience, however, one should keep in mind circumstances that may not apply elsewhere. One of these was the close identification of the writer with the point of view of the agency executive and practitioner staff. The subordination of the research goals to overall agency goals, as indicated in Chapter 2, might not be acceptable to all behavioral scientists. We are neither boastful nor apologetic on this characteristic. We are merely being explicit because it tended to reduce certain goal displacement pressures and to expand others.

In general, the SRS project was rich in pressures of the second type, and relatively poor in those of the first and third types.

The paucity of "empire-building" is seen, in that the SRS consisted of the writer and his secretary at its inception and also at the close of the demonstration. Some of the need for expansion was obviated by having special staff for projects. But the projects were always decentralized. It was hardly an announced goal, or even a matter of formal policy; it was simply a matter of personal preference that the SRS should remain a one-man operation. There was also an awareness that the addition of other persons would add to administrative responsibilities, which were shunned wherever possible.

Thus the writer by his convictions and definition of the research consultant role, became vulnerable less to the first type of goal displacement than to the second—that directed toward getting "quick," superficial results which give the appearance of attainment of the seven goals outlined earlier.

Before reviewing displacement behavior with respect to each of the SRS goals, a distinction should be made between two types of displacement. Type A was characterized by giving inordinate weight to one goal at the expense of one or more of the others, usually of higher priority. Type B, on the other hand, was characterized by substituting goals other than the seven specified, or by substituting the appearance of goal attainment for actual attainment.

The supra-goal of *promoting the client organization's growth*—in effectiveness, not size—was central to the first four enumerated goals. To illustrate: the goal was not simply to encourage careful research (goal 1), but to do so as a means of promoting the organization's effectiveness. Similarly, the improvement of the client organization's community position (goal 4) was to enable it to do a more effective continuing job, rather than for the edification of those who identify with it. When the consultant's effort is directed toward a substitute for improving the organization's effectiveness, then goal displacement has taken place. Here, a key goal is usurped by one of lesser importance, constituting a Type A displacement.

Several instances of Type A displacement came into the situation either as actualities or as potentialities.

There were many instances in which the SRS found itself *doing* things *for* a client organization rather than maintaining a detached consulting relationship so that growth effectiveness would occur through the organization's own activities. This is the all too familiar situation in which the consultant falls into the trap of becoming a doer, which is widely recognized by psychiatrists, social caseworkers, and sophisticated community development workers. In such cases, the consultant preempts the client's right to grow by doing things it might more advantageously do itself, thus encouraging a dependency relationship that hinders rather than promotes growth. The usual pressure for this behavior came through invitations to the SRS to make a study, rather than to help the organization make one.

This kind of goal displacement is more relevant to local-level projects than to state-level ones; for as mentioned earlier, the relation to local-level projects was that of an outside consultant, while the relationship to state level projects was more that of a staff resource. On the state level, it was fitting that the SRS should take major administrative responsibility in some of the studies.

It is apparent in reviewing the seven enumerated SRS goals that any of them may involve goal displacement to the extent that it interferes with the supra-goal of promoting the client organization's growth in effectiveness. The first four are specifically directed to this purpose, while the last three can interfere to the extent that their pursuit makes inroads on the time allotted to the first four.

In actual experience, the first goal of *encouraging research* exerted strong pulls toward Type A displacement. Four ways in which it had a tendency to become an end in itself will be mentioned.

The first occurs when the research investigator spends disproportionate time on projects which interest him for reasons other than the goals for which he is presumably striving. In this instance, he may neglect projects that do not interest him as much, or turn down requests for consulting help because he is "too busy" with his pet projects.

The second involves research becoming not a basis for action but a substitute for action. Agency staff and volunteer citizens often are aware of this possibility; but it nevertheless happens that a research project sometimes legitimates the will not to act. The "one—two—three—Go" can become "three and one-half—three and three-fourths—etc., etc." The tendency is illustrated by the county supervisor who frankly declared that the survey would "get these people off our backs for a while." Often, avoidance of this kind of goal displacement requires that the consultant contact more of the client system, or help recruit a project system to take over implementation. In other instances, he may simply advise that a study is not required in order to move ahead.

A third kind of displacement is the temptation, when organizational factors bog down, to "get the project done" while neglecting the organizational implications. It is both time-saving and ego-enhancing for the consultant to move into stalemated local situations and to take over the responsibility. This may be precisely what is hoped for by parts of the client system.

A fourth displacement is closely related. It is the temptation for the consultant, in order to get the research done, to restrict his contacts only to that part of the client organization which is "for" the project and is willing to work on it, thus neglecting broader contact with the client system which is desirable for growth effectiveness and implementation.

Type B displacements involve the temptation to do superficial research instead of the "real thing," and to do things other than research. Given the research consultant role as developed in Chapter 2, wide latitude in the sophistication of the research designs is permissible, but with the qualification that the limitations of the findings be clearly acknowledged. Within these limits, most competent research consultants would hardly be tempted to water down their procedures still further.

But the temptation to seek approval by engaging in activities other than research is a more ominous pitfall. For there is tremendous pressure on the consultant to do all sorts of pleasant things: make speeches, attend conferences, participate in program planning, keep up his necessary "contacts," be a good fellow, and so on. That such activities may on occasion help to develop further research projects should not be denied. But in affirming it, let the researcher who is also a human being beware. Given the right set of social skills, a person could survive for years in a "Social Research Service" doing almost everything else but bona fide research and consultation.

The second major goal of the SRS was that of *encouraging action in implementing the findings and recommendations of studies.* The most usual Type A displacement involved the consultant in drawing up recommendations from the study findings. Citizens' organizations, particularly where paid staff is not available, may appreciate the chance to unload this responsibility. Often it is accompanied by the well-intentioned "You know so much more about this than we do." In some cases, he may. But in any case this is a sign that he has partially failed to avoid a dependency relationship. The question is, which goal takes precedence: goal 2 or the preamble supra-goal? If he is helping the organization grow in effectiveness, he will avoid encouraging abdication of responsibility. Yet he need not detach himself completely from the process of evolving recommendations. He may meet with a Recommendations Subcommittee, and may make suggestions on a draft of recommendations; he certainly can be of help in pointing out the relation between any proposed recommendation and what the study may have found.

Another Type A displacement of the implementation goal is the obvious one of designing a study that will support a decision already made. An excellent example of this is the tendency of the mental health associations to view their surveys as ammunition for obtaining goals to which they are already committed—the establishment of a County Mental Health Board, mental health outpatients clinics, and so on. In such cases, the implementation goal has become absolute, and the survey project is subordinate to it. While in Chapter 2 it was asserted that research is definitely subordinated to an action outcome, this is not the same as saying that research should be subordinate to a specific decision on an action outcome, taken prior to the research.

In a sense, the above situation approximates the Type B displacement, in which the appearance of goal attainment is substituted for actual goal attainment. Certainly this is the case where a research project is deliberately conceived in order to justify a decision that had already been reached for other reasons. As one scientist, tongue in cheek, has put it,

> Here is my recipe for how to become a famous researcher. Get three clever administrators, place them in one hotel room, mix with one bottle of bourbon, and get them to talk about the things they know are going to have to be done in three years' time. Now go out and devise a research project which proves that these things should be done. In the three years' time that it takes you to do the research, they will already be doing these things themselves. You will then be labeled as a prophet and can retire as a successful researcher.[1]

[1] Comment by John Cumming at the Social Research Conference, June, 1960.

No instances of Type A goal displacement were perceived by the writer with respect to goal 3: *helping the client agency become aware of the behavioral components of its work.*

Type B displacements, however—the appearance of goal attainment as a substitute for actual attainment—are possible regarding goal 3. There is always the temptation to seem to interpret behavioral science concepts and findings, while not really doing so. Strong pressures come from two directions. One is the great interest of practitioners in the health and welfare field to "get scientific answers" to their problems, even where the behavioral sciences are far from having definitive answers. The other is the possible proclivity of the behavioral scientist to yield to social expectations and deliver seemingly authoritative answers when he is speaking on little more than a layman's hunches. He may be pushed by the fear of disappointing his interrogators and pulled by the reward of a willing and appreciative audience. Under such circumstances, the temptation to pontificate is great.

A related displacement is to do things other than communicate valid behavioral science findings. As an example, the writer was invited to give a talk on "The Cultural Aspects of Smoking" at a statewide meeting of health education personnel and agency administrators. Since two research investigators in the field of teenage smoking were on the same program, the writer decided to make his talk general in nature. He pitched it in a whimsical vein as though he were hired to advise the tobacco industry on how to cope with the alleged association between smoking and lung cancer. The talk was extremely well received, but it is questionable how much real communication of valid behavioral science findings had taken place. There was also apprehension on the part of the writer that he was getting a name for being "an interesting speaker" for sessions of that type, a function he did not care to perform.

Sure enough, the next year he was again invited to give a paper to the same group: this time on "The Structure and Function of Communities." To put to rest any possible reputation as a light entertainer, he delivered a rather involved paper on the topic without concessions to the audience either of interest or intelligibility. Any possible misconception that he could be relied upon to give an interesting but harmless talk spiced with a few scientific or pseudo-scientific observations was abruptly removed. But it was once more doubtful how much communication of behavioral science had taken place. In both instances, the goal had been largely displaced.

The fourth goal is deliberately a subordinate one—that of *helping client organizations improve their position in the community*. This goal had two applications to the SRS demonstration. The presence of the research consultant and the development of a research project often gave support to the local organization. As a simple example, when a local Health Association was able to make the SRS available to an interagency committee, the act enhanced the position of the Health Association in the community. Likewise a state association, in securing the services of the SRS for a local affiliate, also found its hand somewhat strengthened.

During this period some local health associations were involved in a fund-raising controversy with their United Funds. In this situation Type A displacement might take place, for example, by requesting the SRS to help with "market research" whose results might put the local affiliate in a stronger position tactically, or through soliciting consultation on how to promote the organization's interests in the controversy. Both types of request were made—each only once—and both were declined. Declining the advice function is described on page 49. The reason given for declining the market research was that "this type of project should be conducted by a commercial organization, not by the SCAA's Social Research Service."

The fifth and sixth goals related to *developing new research techniques or findings which would be of significance to others than the client organization*. To the extent that this was carried out, there seemed to be little goal displacement, with one exception.

An idea for the study of characteristics of health service recipients originated in discussion with a behavioral scientist from the State Health Department. (See page 125.) It was believed to be a way of moving ahead in an important aspect of research evaluation—to answer the question: Are you reaching the people you purport to be reaching? It was believed that the findings would have broad program significance (goal 6), and that a methodology could be evolved in such a study which might be useful elsewhere (goal 5).

The choice of a county was determined solely on the basis of convenience for the research, and negotiations with the county organizations were motivated by the goal of getting the research done. Action implementation was ignored except for the intent to make the findings available to other agencies.

As a result, the research was foisted on a less than enthusiastic (though cooperative) Health Association. The principal contacts with the Association and the Health Department were not broadly based. And the possible relationship of the project to the Council of Social Agencies was completely neglected. This last might have upset the project, had it not been for the acquaintance of the writer with the Council's executive.

This was clearly a Type A displacement, where perfectly justifiable goals (goals 5 and 6) were pursued as absolutes, and not within the overall rubric of the preamble.

Type B displacements—or substituting the appearance of goal attainment for actual attainment—for goals 5 and 6 do not appear to be particularly applicable, and so far as is known did not take place.

The seventh goal was that of *encouraging the utilization of research in health and welfare agencies* throughout New York State and in other parts of the country. Two preliminary observations provide perspective for this goal. The first is that the SCAA as a statewide citizens' organization has always exercised a function of working toward improvements in practice—through the demonstration of new methods, through public or professional education, through services to public and voluntary agencies, and through legislative activities. The new SRS operated within this tradition. The second is that the SRS itself was conceived as a "demonstration" project, whose possible usefulness was not only to the SCAA, but to show what benefits might be applicable in analogous settings.

Type A displacement would involve the pursuit of the goal of encouraging research utilization to the extent of interfering with the other six goals. There were occasions on which considerable effort was spent in connection with this goal, but apparently Type A displacement did not take place.

Type B displacement was relevant in at least one important respect. During the period of the demonstration, considerable progress was made toward the development of social research functions throughout the state. It would be easy for the SRS, which worked deliberately toward this goal, to take more than its share of credit for the increase. This would involve Type B displacement, in that the developments offer the "appearance" of goal attainment by the SRS. Attributing them to the SRS involved, logically, the *post hoc, ergo propter hoc* fallacy: I worked to bring it about. It came about. Therefore, I brought it about.

This point is worth making, for it is all too apparent that this type of goal displacement—assuming credit for an event with *post hoc, ergo propter hoc* reasoning—is widespread in the field of health and welfare activities. It is one reason that the application of adequate methods of evaluational research is so greatly needed.

Closely related is another Type B displacement. One perhaps could have been effective in "selling" social research by encouraging questionable hopes for its ability both to produce short-run results and to accomplish short-run goals. The danger of making unrealistic promises of "results" is obvious. But being overly sanguine as to the particular ends which social research will serve is equally hazardous. For encouraging the idea that "research" can give easy answers, not only to the substantive but also to the value problems involved, is well beyond the present state of our knowledge of human behavior, and must be only self-defeating in the long run.

We have considered displacement in relation to each of the seven SRS goals. In closing, let us consider it briefly in connection with all goals taken in aggregate. Type A displacement, by definition, does not apply. But Type B displacement is pertinent and warrants brief summary.

In what respects did the SRS substitute other goals than the seven specified ones, or substitute the appearance of goal attainment for actual goal attainment? Earlier in the chapter it was indicated that displacement pressures in the direction of "empire-building" were not great, nor were displacement pressures in the direction of substituting the writer's personal research program and strategy for that called for by the SRS' announced goals. Pressure toward goal displacement from the program interests of the field staff, by contrast, was a constant stimulus of which the writer was aware.

Let us be clearer about these pressures. They were in the direction of diverting the SRS' activities from the seven goals to activities more directly related to program development—which understandably was the principal concern of the field staff. They saw the writer not only as a social research resource, but as a resource for program purposes not necessarily connected with the seven goals; for example, making speeches at meetings, performing community organization functions, "trouble-shooting," and working on substantive material in the health and welfare field. In quite a direct sense, they were pressures to become a practitioner, rather than a researcher or consultant.

As mentioned earlier, the researcher can, if he is not careful, find his time frittered away by pleasant and often rewarding "busy-work" activities that have the aura of relevance to his position but actually contribute little or nothing to goal attainment. Talking with people who drop in, keeping up with what colleagues are doing, conferring on general agency matters rather than on specific research matters, attending conferences—the situation is not, of course, unique to researchers—constitute a pleasant, and in part necessary, kind of "treading water." Some of these activities also earn good will and approval from one's associates, professional colleagues, and citizens' groups. Indeed, hour for hour, time spent in this sort of busy-work and in "public relations" types of contact with field workers and local groups yields perhaps a higher output of approval and good will than time spent in bona fide research consultation and other research activities.

In this type of goal displacement, energy that presumably might go into goal attainment behavior instead becomes drained off into "system-maintenance" behavior. A large bureaucracy may not be involved; nevertheless, the research investigator finds himself "working for the organization" rather than for the attainment of its goals.

5. Goal Attainment and Goal Failure

IN CONSIDERING the Social Research Service a "demonstration," the following components were involved:

1. A new kind of service, not previously available, was to be introduced into the State Charities Aid Association.

2. Since the value of the service had not been established, the agency would be relieved of the financial outlay for providing the service during the time in which it was being developed and assessed: it was financed during the period by Russell Sage Foundation.

3. The SCAA would then assess whether the service was worthwhile.

4. If the service was found to be worthwhile, it would become incorporated into the permanent structure of the agency.

5. Presumably, the experience gained in the demonstration would be of use to other agencies in helping them determine the extent to which an analogous service might be useful to them.

Performance and Effectiveness of Functions

One general test of the success or failure of the project would be the agency's decision as to whether the "demonstrated" service was sufficiently worthwhile for it to continue the service and pay the bill for it. A favorable decision was made by the SCAA's governing Board on the recommendation of its Long-Range Planning Committee at the end of the second year of the demonstration.

In an empirical sense, then, the SRS demonstration was "successful." But this decision by the Board, though relevant and reassuring, can hardly be used as a criterion of overall assessment of the SRS.

In the first place, it is an all-or-none verdict; whereas one should be skeptical about assuming that any operation can be totally successful or a total failure.

In the second place, the decision itself does not provide the basis on which the judgment was made. If the SRS was worth continuing, why was it? And despite what?

If the demonstration experience is to be of value to others, the assessment must be specific, and in relative degree, rather than by all-or-none decision. To this end, the seven goals outlined in the preceding chapter will be useful. We shall see that:

1. Goal attainment and goal failure were experienced in differing degrees, with respect to all seven goals.

2. Some goals were given a higher priority than others and had greater direct bearing on the specific projects attempted.

3. Both goal attainment and goal failure were typically not so much an end result as a process which began with the inception of each project.

Encouraging Research

Two kinds of goal attainment are indicated by the questions: To what extent were the activities carried out? To what extent were they effective? In connection with the first goal of *encouraging research as a basis for program planning and operation*, the first question is best answered by reviewing the list of project activities in Chapter 1 (and described briefly in Appendix B). Most are clearly program-oriented research.

The question of the effectiveness of the activities can be viewed from whether the research projects were brought to a satisfactory conclusion, yielding valid findings, and whether action was taken to initiate or modify programs as a result of the findings and recommendations.

Of the principal projects listed in Chapter 1, the epidemiological study of tuberculosis patients as a research project fell somewhere between goal attainment and goal failure. The basic data were gathered and analyzed, but the Committee did not complete the work of preparing a formal report, or of evolving a set of recommendations.

The major county mental health surveys all were completed and resulted in carefully prepared reports with recommendations. In some instances, however, the contribution of the consultant was minimal, being confined to one or two contacts. Nonetheless, the episodes were numerous and should not be ignored.

The screening device for multi-problem families was carried through the original test with 50 multi-problem families and 50 control families. Preliminary statistical analyses were made, but the projected item analysis and revision of the scale had not been carried through at this writing.

The research-demonstration project with multi-problem families was developed into a concrete project proposal; funds were obtained from the Social Security Administration, and a three-year project was put into operation. At the time of writing, March, 1962, it had been in operation for many months; the project system was firmly established, and research and case-work staffs were at work.

Field work was completed on the study of characteristics of health service recipients, and analysis of the findings was now under way. Reports were scheduled for the State Health Conference, both by behavior scientists and by the health commissioner.

The study of county health services in X County was brought to a successful conclusion with publication of some of the findings in a state medical journal.

Although the design, screening instrument, and plans for the entire project of identifying tuberculosis patients likely to become recalcitrant were completed, the project itself was not undertaken for a variety of reasons, ranging from the death of the county health commissioner and resignation of the Health Association executive director to lack of continuing interest.

There were numerous additional minimal-contact projects at the county level. Approximately one-third of them did not result in an actual study. The remainder culminated in a study either completed or well under way at this writing. In most of these cases, the SRS was able to give presumably helpful service.

Among the state-level projects, the study of county health and welfare needs was brought to a conclusion, as described in Chapter 3. A formal report was issued, which had wide circulation.

The "Youth in Custody" Studies were concluded and resulted in a two-part report.

The Statewide Adoption Survey involved a grant of funds from two foundations. It had its own staff, to which the SRS gave general consulting aid. The study was completed and a report of major proportions published. The adoptability study was brought to a conclusion and was published as a separate report.

The project to develop a document descriptive of current projects with multi-problem families in New York State was completed and the results published.

County Profiles was published and widely distributed, followed by a revised and enlarged edition, *County and City Profiles*. In addition, the state tuberculosis staff requested that the SRS prepare separate textual profiles of approximately eight counties in which it made administrative evaluations.

The Christmas Seal Study design was worked out by an educational psychologist with considerable participation from the SRS. Administrative decisions, involving both finances and policy, resulted in its not yet being activated.

As with the local projects, there were several state-level projects of smaller research significance, such as helping the State Heart Assembly design forms for the systematic reporting of cases examined in its cardiac evaluation centers, and helping the State Committee on Children and Public Welfare devise forms for a self-study. Their eventual outcome presumably was influenced only minimally by the SRS.

So far we have considered the first goal from the standpoint of projects which actually were undertaken, and whether or not they were brought to a satisfactory research conclusion.

But a pertinent point is implicit in the last clause of the goal: helping to impart attitudes and techniques for critical factual evaluation. This relates mostly to the SCAA itself, to its allied statewide organizations, and to the county-level affiliates.

Many factors contributed to the change in structure and function of the SCAA during the demonstration period, but perhaps the most dynamic was the nationwide fund-raising controversy between the independent health associations and the United Funds. In New York State the controversy permeated the SCAA through the activities of its allied organizations. Briefly, the SCAA entered this period as a service organization, organically tied to its allied statewide organizations. It emerged with a relationship of informal cooperation substituted for the formal ties. SCAA now exercises an influence on state health and welfare activities in its own right, rather than through the initiative of its allied organizations. It has a central staff of specialized ability free to collaborate with any organization, and with a pattern of collaborating in action-oriented studies or in research-demonstrations in the health and welfare fields.

It is impossible to assign valid quantitative weights to the factors in this change. There seems to be agreement, however, that the Social Research Service was an important element in two ways: (1) in constituting itself a model, however imperfect, of expert service—if a Social Research Service could become useful, so perhaps could a Chronic Disability Service, and so perhaps could other new salients in staff development; (2) in being of direct aid to the Long-Range Planning Committee by conducting the health and welfare needs study that uncovered the need for community health service consultation.

There is little question also that the executive staff of SCAA acquired a lively interest in social research, both to assess program development and to evaluate new programs. A rewarding experience for the writer was to hear the executive director inform a worker in the mental health field that the SCAA would not be interested in cooperating with a certain project unless its impact were to be evaluated by research.

With regard to the first goal, one might summarize by saying that a number of research projects were developed and carried through both on the state and county levels. Others were not brought to a successful conclusion, either because the advisability of pursuing them did not seem great, or because in one way or another they faltered or failed in the process. Nonetheless, there was clear evidence that favorable attitudes toward critical evaluation had been encouraged and strengthened, although there was something less than full commitment on the part of all state and local organizations.

Encouraging Implementation

The second goal was encouraging *action in implementing the studies involved.* In considering this goal there are two questions of evaluation: what activities actually were undertaken to further the goal, and to what extent was the goal attained?

It is not exaggeration to report that with one deliberate exception, no extensive relationship developed in any project without eventual implementation being considered from the outset. This was true because of the stated policy of the SRS, and the writer's acceptance of implementation as a legitimate goal, even with higher priority than that of adding to theoretical knowledge.

The focus of the consultant was continuously on the structure of the project system so that legitimation of implementation would come about as part of the project episode, rather than be added at the project's end. (See Chapter 3.) Thus, usually at the first meeting processes were set in motion to induce structural changes that would establish both a viable project system for making the study and further legitimation of its implementation.

On the statewide level, projects varied from great to only modest implementation. Obviously, the Long-Range Planning study of health and welfare needs had direct implementation by utilizing the findings to initiate a major new program, and by inadvertently contributing to adaptive changes in the SCAA's structure and function.

The Statewide Adoption Survey involved the setting up of a prestigious *ad hoc* committee, with a view toward legitimation and eventual implementation. Likewise, data-gathering efforts on the local level were structured to encourage the development of local project systems to assure not only the needed state data but local implementation as well. As in the local mental health surveys, local-level data gathering was encouraged at some cost in effi-

ciency but with intent of gathering dividends from later implementation. It is difficult to assess in any rigorous way how much
increased local activity would have occurred without the use of
local committees, but using, somewhat impressionistically, the
method of considering these counties as their own "controls"—
that is, of comparing what was being done in adoption services
during the year or two before the study with what was done
throughout and after the study—there is indication of increased
activity.

As this account was written, the report of the adoption study
was in press. It provides a rich source of information on the
extent of difficulties in the adoption situation. In the writer's
estimation, it will probably not be followed through by the State
Committee on Adoption, as an action group, although it doubtless will be used by the local groups. Part of the reason is that it
was never explicitly stated as a goal that this Committee itself
should take implementational action. The close relation of the
study to the State Association of Councils and Chests and to the
SCAA was such that they could take statewide action in their
own right.

The Youth in Custody study apparently produced limited
action on both the local and state levels. Its findings were put to
use by the State Committee on Children and Public Welfare in
communicating with legislators and departments of the state
government regarding recommended changes. It received wide
newspaper coverage—the widest of any effort in the recent
history of the SCAA. Alert reporters frequently interviewed local
officials on the unfavorable conditions which the study had found
and thus brought the matters to public attention. Some local
committees that had engaged in data-gathering took follow-up
action—in one instance, to establish a county probation service,
in another to improve detention facilities, and so on.

At the state level, although the reports and recommendations
provided the State Committee on Children and Public Welfare
with a platform for action to improve treatment of young offenders in New York State, no major implementation was effected.
This would have taken considerable effort, which, of course, was

beyond the acceptable role of the SRS to initiate. (Let it be noted, parenthetically, that the writer's disappointment may be associated with the fact, as indicated in Chapter 2, that it was he who had conceived the study and drafted the policy recommendations to the State Committee. Perhaps had he taken less initiative in these matters, the State Committee might have taken more in implementation.)

Implementation of local projects also was varied. Of the three mental health surveys in which major consultation was afforded, two proceeded to the successful establishment of a County Mental Health Board. The third is being used as part of another county's campaign action toward this objective. Greater success apparently attends the use of survey findings for this purpose than for program modifications in the mental health associations themselves.

Of the local health studies which were completed, perhaps half had some appreciable action outcome. In some instances, however, the intervention of the SRS was so minimal that favorable or unfavorable action outcome is hardly relevant to its goal attainment or failure.

The research demonstration project with Multi-Problem Families had at the time of writing just been launched on a three-year term, although a long sequence of development and planning preceded it. The expectation is that if the casework unit proves its value, it will be carried on as a permanent resource. The active participation on the planning body of the chairman and several members of the Welfare Committee of the County Board of Supervisors, the Welfare Commissioner, and officials from the State Department of Social Welfare indicate that a viable foundation is established for subsequent action.

In summary, considerable implementation of findings or recommendations from completed studies has occurred on both the state and local levels, ranging from extensive to extremely minimal. On both levels, also, inadvertent changes in structure and function were occasioned by many projects, invariably in the direction of strengthening the organization, if sometimes only modestly. One might conclude that about as much implementation occurred as might reasonably be expected, with enough failures and misfires to remind the faint of heart that such efforts are not likely to be uniformly rewarding.

Encouraging Greater Awareness of Behavioral Components

The goal of *helping the client organizations acquire a greater awareness of the behavioral components of their work* was clearly considered to be of less importance than those of encouraging research and action implementation. Nevertheless, it was anticipated that the consultant would serve as a bridge to the behavioral sciences, introducing concepts and findings which would be helpful to the organizations in taking a more analytical view of their work.

The two areas of knowledge most frequently tapped were those associated with the dynamics of community action, and with the behavior of people whom program developments were designed to benefit. The first included somewhat elementary briefing on community structure and function; introducing material on community leadership and power structures; considering projects as instances of community actions (much in the manner of Chapter 3, but less systematically); and looking at the relation of project process to possible implementation. The second had to do with "fit" between agency programs and their prospective recipients, particularly around considerations of motivation, value priorities, subcultural differences and social class differences.

It may be recalled from Chapter 1 that research devoted to the internal structure of organizations—the field of organizational theory—was specifically excluded from the consultant's role as developed by the writer. Attention was to be given to the project system rather than to the formal organizations in relation to which the project system emerged.

In retrospect, it appears that this important body of knowledge should not have been neglected. For attention devoted to the formal organization of these citizens' associations in respect to their manifest goals might have great potential for improvement in effectiveness. At very best, it might have helped organizations to examine and reorganize themselves as part of a dynamic interaction process.

It is difficult to assess how much was conveyed or how much increased understanding was facilitated by the SRS. Certainly, there was little naive faith that knowledge could be derived automatically from participation in the survey process. In fact, a Michigan state study of a community health self-survey had specifically underscored the inadequacy of any expectation that self-surveys, because they involve citizen participation, will automatically yield increments of educational attainment.[1]

A quotation from the consultant's notes in the course of one mental health survey illustrates the way the educational goal may bog down:

> The educational process which is usually thought of as a desirable concomitant of a survey is not taking place because the data gatherers have been given no conception of where their part fits into the total operation, or why the material they are gathering is important. No attention has been given by either the Society's Board or by its Survey Committee to considering what it is trying to do and why, and what it will all mean when it is done. . . .
>
> I believe that an early meeting of all people who have participated in the survey or who are interested in it could be of great value. This meeting would be an occasion for considering once again why a survey was thought wise in the first place, what purposes it was hoped would be accomplished by it, and more specifically, the way in which particular material being gathered will be useful both for the local association and for the county as a whole in its planning for services in the mental health field.

At the time this was written, the writer was still oriented to the field staff's taking major responsibility for this activity, but a meeting as outlined was arranged at which his suggestion was carried out. In later projects, largely as a result of similar experiences, the consultant gradually assumed more initiative *vis-à-vis* the field staff in the organizational and educational aspects.

Thus, particularly after the role change described in Chapter 2, the consultant not only introduced pertinent information in the

[1] Sower, Christopher, and others, *Community Involvement: The Webs of Formal and Informal Ties That Make for Action.* The Free Press, Glencoe, Ill., 1957.

consulting situations that arose, but at times took the initiative to plan for meetings in which these aspects of the process were considered.

A similar process of continuous, but not particularly intensive, activity was carried on at the state level in relation to administrative staffs. That is, social science knowledge was introduced largely in an *ad hoc* fashion; almost always in relation to a specific situation rather than for its own sake, and usually in nontechnical terms.

Another form of communicating social science knowledge was through formal "papers" and speeches delivered by the author at annual meetings and other special occasions. Lists of the more important papers and speeches are given in Appendices D and E. Within the SCAA's allied organizations, the health organizations were the principal ones to show initiative in asking for talks regarding the social sciences. They usually had specific problems in mind, and expected that the behavioral sciences could afford relevant and helpful material.

No attempt was made to measure the impact of such speeches and papers. Generally, they were enthusiastically received, which in itself indicates—but certainly does not assure—that they may have had some impact.

A minor attempt to involve the SCAA's Board of Managers was a clear failure. Early in the demonstration the writer prepared a brief memorandum on "Social Changes Affecting the SCAA." It enumerated not so much any basic changes taking place in American society, as certain more immediate changes in the state and local, government and voluntary institutional structures through which health and welfare services are administered in New York State. The thought was expressed that the memorandum might be helpful, perhaps to the Long-Range Planning Committee, or the administrative staff, or to the Board as a whole, in reviewing the current situation and the present and possible roles of the SCAA in it. The memorandum was included among other materials distributed at a Board meeting, with supporting comments by the executive director. But no action was taken by the staff or the Board to utilize it as a basis for long-range planning. There simply was too wide a gap between the trends outlined therein and the pragmatic, agenda-oriented formal action which the Board usually takes.

One can summarize, then, that the principal activities taken toward helping client organizations acquire a greater awareness of the behavioral components of their work consisted of informally introducing pertinent material into consulting situations at which specific issues were being considered, and through occasional formal speeches and papers. This minor goal is believed to have been attained modestly in both ways.

Secondary Goals

A goal that was almost marginal was that of *helping the client organizations improve their general position in the community*. This goal was advanced incidentally through other activities—chiefly those of engaging in research and implementing it. Nonetheless, there were a few occasions on which an action was taken with this goal principally in mind.

How could the activities of the SRS contribute to the improvement of the position of the client organizations? First, the eligibility of the client organization for access to this service—to be in a position to make it available—was a source of prestige to some. For example, a health field representative's report commented, "Sally (the local executive secretary) was loud in her praise of Dr. W.'s help in their Mental Health survey. He gave them just what they needed. She seemed so pleased to be able to offer a valuable service to the community. Now, they look to her for guidance." It should also be realized that in some upstate New York counties, to be able to produce a "real, flesh-and-blood social scientist" who had "written a book" constituted an important achievement for a local organization. Even in many larger cities, the ability to have the SRS available in a consultant role in a discussion of an interagency project constituted an "asset" for the local organization.

A more substantial source of improvement of the organization's community position was often the research project which occasioned the consultation. That the organization was conducting a research project had its prestigious aspects, especially in light of the current status values that "research" activities enjoy among practitioner agencies. Superficially, of course, this can lead toward goal displacement. But an organization that has produced a good piece of useful research in line with its program objectives is often understandably accorded respect.

As a related point, many surveys of even modest nature help to put the local organization in a position where people feel "it knows whereof it speaks." If the organization has just completed a survey of local conditions, it can have a little more assurance that it will have a respectful hearing from the city council, the county board of supervisors, the press, and from the other agencies of the community. In addition, a "halo effect" spreads from the particular subject matter on which it is adjudged competent to other more or less related matters.

The above applied also to the relationship of the SRS to the SCAA and its allied state organizations. As a result of several projects, the sponsoring organizations could not only speak more authoritatively within the areas of the specific project, but gained authority throughout the related field.

Finally, the ability of the SCAA to provide a research consultant, and to have someone who could prepare papers on topics such as those listed in Appendix D, was a modest source of prestige to it. The two areas in which the position of SCAA was noticeably strengthened were the promotion of research in other health and welfare agencies, and the shaping of public policy with respect to the rehabilitative aspects of public welfare.

The remaining three goals relate to a wider circle than just the client organizations. It was hoped—perhaps as a by-product of particular episodes of research—that *tools, methods, and procedures might be developed which would be useful elsewhere in New York State and the country.*

In only one instance was this a primary goal—the study of characteristics of health service recipients. It was felt that this project could pioneer an evaluational methodology, to help agencies answer the question: Are you reaching the people you purport to be reaching? It is hoped that the study methodology will be of help to other organizations, particularly to welfare councils in making studies of welfare and health services. Two papers were prepared for presentation at the State Health Conference; one on the methodology, and one on the study findings.

Another contribution to methodology may come from the design and implementation of the research-demonstration project with multi-problem families, which has involved knotty problems of adapting control-group designs to field research. A paper was presented to the Research Section of the National Conference on Social Welfare on the methodology of this project. There have been numerous requests for copies of the design, and for help with questions from others contemplating similar research.

A further attempt to devise a tool of broad usefulness was that in connection with the development of a screening device for early identification of tuberculosis patients who have high potential for recalcitrance. This project, however, was never implemented. Another instance was the development of a screening device for multi-problem families. Although the first stages of this project developed satisfactorily, the project was discontinued, at least temporarily, for reasons beyond the control of the SRS.

Within the organizations served by the SRS, two tools served additional usefulness. One was *County and City Profiles* which became the basis for local data-books, and aided staff evaluational studies of local county health associations. The other was the outline for mental health surveys, which was used several times in New York State and in at least two instances in other states.

Hence, this fifth goal, an explicitly subsidiary one, was modestly attained.

A related goal was *the obtaining of study findings which would have program implications elsewhere in New York State and in other parts of the country.*

The study of characteristics of health service recipients and the research-demonstration with multi-problem families are both projects which may arouse general interest in their findings as well as methodology. Interest in the statewide study of adoption is also likely to spread to pertinent groups throughout the country.

Some indication of general interest is provided by the number of requests that came from other parts of the United States for special publications as a result of their mention in journals or through word of mouth. As of March, 1962, the number of requests for these reports, over and above an extensive initial mailing of each of them, is indicated below.

Youth in Custody	179
County Profiles	244
Health and Welfare Needs in New York State	115
Multi-Problem Families: A New Name or A New Problem?	1,477

In some cases, additional requests could not be filled because the supply was exhausted.

It would seem that this sixth goal was also attained to a moderate extent.

A final goal was *to encourage similar utilization of research in other health and welfare organizations throughout New York State and in other parts of the country.*

Many forces converged to further this same end, making it difficult to assess what the SRS may have contributed to it. First, was the generally increased activity in applied social research in the fields of marketing, industrial research, and organizational research, as well as in health and welfare. Second, was the increasing cry for more effective preventive and restorative measures in public welfare with an accompanying stimulus to applied research. Third, was the increased consciousness of the inadequacy of mere annual-report accountability to the public for the value of the work that agencies are doing. And finally, there was the continued development of research techniques and methodologies, and a growing availability of private and public funds for research activities in health and welfare. The establishment of research grant programs in the Social Security Administration and the Children's Bureau was an important stimulus to such research.

A few specific activities of the SRS may have had some stimulus value in the development of research activities in New York State. These include numerous conversations or consultations with various welfare department commissioners and welfare council executives. Several papers read before state organizations pointing out research needs and possibilities in varied fields may also have had some effectiveness.

Two activities should be mentioned in particular. One was the publication on Multi-Problem Families, which received wide circulation and apparently served as a stimulus to research undertakings in a number of instances. The most notable direct effect was the development of the research-demonstration project in Chemung County, which in turn served to increase interest in this type of research demonstration.

The other specific activity was the conference on Social Research in the Development of Health and Welfare Agency Programs. This conference was specifically designed to promote agency-based research. It resulted in a document which has had wide circulation, and it set in motion discussions which later came to fruition in the Chemung County project and also contributed to the development of a research function in the State Welfare Department.

On a more inclusive scale, it is anticipated that the present volume, in its attempt to report frankly on the SRS demonstration and to conceptualize the results of the experience, may serve as an aid to those who are considering research.

Time and Priorities

One question is pertinent not only to the review of goal attainment and goal failure, but to the earlier discussions of the research consultant role and of social research projects as social action episodes. This is the question of the degree of initiative that should be exercised by the consultant. From the present account it will be apparent that some projects which "never got off the ground" might have done so had the consultant been willing to assume greater initiative in developing them and getting the necessary procedures established. Other projects that did get started, but were not completed, might have been completed with increased participation by the consultant. The same is true of projects that were completed but resulted in little or no implementation.

Should increased initiative have been exercised in these instances? There is no blanket answer, for circumstances vary in the relation of the behavioral scientist to the agency and to the goals and goal priorities within which he operates. Nonetheless, let us consider the consultant's initiative at various stages in the projects.

Obviously, it would be foolish for the consultant to assume that every initial contact with a local group concerning a research project should result in a full-blown project. There may be very little real interest by the local group. Or the group may be interested, but unable to expend the resources in money or manpower which a worthwhile project would involve.

Likewise, a project, though started, may become bogged down. Should the consultant make every effort to keep it going? Part of his decision may be based on whether or not he feels that the project system is capable of carrying the project through with additional help from him. But he must also consider whether the probable outcome is worth the additional effort it will require. Often, particularly in smaller projects without special staff, the bogging down may in itself reveal basic weaknesses in the structure of the group, which, it will be recalled, is typically an *ad hoc* structure devised for carrying through the project. The consultant may be aware of defects in communication within the organization, of preempted leadership, of opposing factions, and so on. Often, it may be easier for him to "get the project over the hump" if he narrows his interaction to but a small part of the project system, namely, to the study system itself. And in some cases, he may find it more efficient to deal with an even smaller group of more active and capable people within the study system. Should he do so?

There is a similar question with regard to implementation. In the SRS demonstration, several completed projects resulted in only a modicum of implementation, which conceivably might have been expanded with greater participation by the consultant. Since implementation is an explicit goal, the consultant has at least a partial responsibility for participation leading to implementation.

An obvious example of what might be considered appropriate behavior for the consultant is for him to help in interpreting to local groups how the project was conducted and the meaning of its findings. A less obvious decision is to what extent he should help "sell" the implementing recommendations to strategic parties. The present consultant interpreted his role as not extending to the latter area, but others may make a different assessment. At any rate, there still remains the question of the extent to which it is appropriate for the consultant to advise on how the implementation might take place, what types of structures might channel this action, and so on. This is a question related to the question of the transformation of the project system. (See page 88.)

In all the questions presented above there are two underlying considerations. The first, and more difficult, has to do with the consultant's conception of his proper role, which in turn is related to the setting of goals and goal priorities. No definitive resolution of the problem will be sought here. Let it simply be stated that the seven goals as described and analyzed, constituted, in retrospect, a reasonably good "fit" to the actual experience. Were the present consultant to "do it over again," he would start with the seven goals as described in Chapter 4, and would conceive of his role substantially as described in Chapter 2. He might, however, function more effectively on the basis of the present conceptualization of the experience.

The second consideration relates to the allocation of time. While the preceding analysis has considered the appropriateness of an intervention, assuming that time is available, some projects will "fail" to attain certain goals when they might have succeeded if the consultant had had more time to invest in them. Thus what appears as the failure of one or another goal may be simply the result of a considered decision to invest time in one place rather than another. Almost any type of productive work involves analogous problems of the optimal allocation of time for the greatest aggregate movement in the desired direction.

6. Conclusions

THE PRINCIPAL PURPOSE of this book has been to communicate the experience of the SRS demonstration to social scientists and administrators who are interested in the application of research consultation to voluntary citizens' organizations and social agencies. With this end in view, details have been provided to help the reader understand the SRS setting and to appraise the extent to which statements from it may apply to other situations.

In this chapter, we shall summarize in a somewhat didactic manner those statements that seem worth repeating for critical evaluation and possible use by others.

The Research Consultant Role

Since the research consultant role is not yet precisely defined, a possible source of difficulty lies in the varied orientations toward it which the behavioral scientist and practitioner have.

Different conceptions and expectations may arise because of the different subcultures in which practitioner and scientist participate. Consequently, the most useful consultant will not only be competent in behavioral science knowledge and practices but have a close acquaintance with the practitioner field in which he is operating.

Since there are wide differences in orientation toward research and practice among both practitioners and behavioral scientists, it is unwise to assume that because one individual looks at the relationship in a given way, others of the same discipline will look at it the same way. Hence, it is critically important when initiating a particular staff or consulting relationship to explore the areas of overlap and difference in the respective expectations.

131

The staff role of research consultant can be analyzed in terms of the activities of encouraging research, consulting on projects, interpreting scientific method and behavioral science findings, and functioning as a member of the administrative team.

The activity of encouraging research can be looked upon as a social process which takes place within a set of evolving relationships between scientist and practitioner. The successful "negotiation" of an adequate research design often depends as much on the social processes and relationships that develop as on the strictly substantive and methodological aspects of the projected research.

Two opposing orientations can be differentiated among behavioral scientists who act as research consultants. One places emphasis on the theoretical significance or methodology of the research project as an end in itself. The other emphasizes the utilization of knowledge and techniques as means to serve the program interests of the specific organization. While not mutually exclusive, the two emphases inevitably require that a decision be made to favor one or the other. The present demonstration favored the second.

When encouraging research, one often encounters differences of meaning for the concept of "evaluation." The usual practitioner concept is that of assessing a program against accepted professional standards and procedures, while the behavioral science concept applies rigorous measures to the impact of the program on those whom it allegedly serves.

Since there may be many requests for the research consultant's services, he almost invariably faces a decision whether to offer consultation to all who request it as best he can; or through developmental initiative and selectivity to pursue a certain "research strategy."

Inasmuch as the development of a project is not only a methodological and substantive process but also a social process, the consultant almost always faces a decision as to how much responsibility he will take for the social process. Most projects considered here had their reason-for-being in providing new knowledge for altering programs. Hence, the method of eventual implementation, or "action follow-up," is pertinent to the nature of the study design itself. Both in connection with preparing to conduct the study and to implement its recommendations, the research consultant finds himself dealing not only with research methodology, but with helping the client organization structure itself appropriately.

Interpreting behavioral science findings and methods can be thought of as a "bridge" in which the consultant serves as intermediary between the client and the behavioral science disciplines. The "bridge" function is essentially a teaching function. Scientific competence is not necessarily accompanied by the competence to transmit behavioral science material meaningfully to lay and practitioner groups. The "bridge" function may involve behaviors ranging from formal papers, talks, briefings, consultations, and so on, to routine day-to-day conversations in which constant interpretation and reinterpretation take place.

Lay persons tend to generalize a relatively unknown discipline from their experience with individuals engaged in it. They blur the distinction between behavioral science, on the one hand, and what a particular behavioral scientist does or says, on the other. Personality quirks, related competencies or incompetencies, offhand empirical judgments—all may be projected to the entire field, unless the behavioral scientist offers distinction and clarification.

In functioning as a member of the administrative team, two roles of the behavioral scientist may become confused. One concerns the special contribution which he can make as a behavioral scientist. The other concerns the more diffuse contribution which he may make merely as an intelligent, experienced, and knowledgeable person.

As a member of the administrative team, the behavioral scientist's effectiveness may be related to the status he occupies in the organization, which in turn may be largely affected by the planning that took place as the position was set up.

In consultation with client organizations, the consultant may have the status not only of a behavioral scientist, but of an outsider, a central staff person, a prestige figure, and an individual.

Pressures which deflect him from the performance of his legitimate professional roles include expectations that he will engage excessively in community organization or field consultant activities; that he will function as an "expert" in the subject matter of the research project; that he will make speeches and take on other functions ordinarily performed by a headquarters official, and that he will assume major administrative responsibility for a project rather than offer consultation.

As developed in the SRS demonstration, the research consultant role is that of a professional person who is helping groups become more effective through the utilization of the research process. The appropriate activities as such, are broader than mere consultation on technical aspects of the research. At the same time, they are not so broad as to constitute general consultation to the client system.

The research consultant is a professional person acting in relationship to a client organization, who attempts to promote the organization's growth in effectiveness of structure and function through the utilization of research as a means of gaining knowledge about the program aspects of the organization's environment, and of inducing dynamic social processes to effect adaptation and change within the organization.

Social Research Projects
as Social Action Episodes

Social research projects constitute episodes of social action which can be analyzed in much the same way as other social action episodes.

The social action aspects of research projects are important because they have a bearing on whether the research task itself can be accomplished, on whether the research findings will be used as a basis for action, and on deliberate or inadvertent changes which may occur in the researching organization during the project.

As social action episodes, research projects often involve the setting up of a special *ad hoc* action system to conduct the research and implement the findings, whose structure and function change during the development of the project.

It is possible to accommodate all the consultation episodes of the SRS demonstration in a general model whose principal attributes are italicized in the paragraph below.

> A research project is a *social action episode* involving *task accomplishment* (including both the *research* and its *implementation*), in which a *consultant* enters into a relationship with a *client system*, out of which is set up a *project system*. Both of these systems undergo *planned and unplanned changes* as the tasks of research and implementation are attempted.

Since the reason-for-being of such research projects lies in the implementation of program modifications, both research and implementation are relevant considerations at all stages of the project.

As the consultant enters into a relationship with a group for research consultation, an important task is to determine what group actually constitutes the client system. He also will need to decide what parts of the client system he should relate to—what parts can "speak for" the system, and what parts can or should interact with him on behalf of the system.

Three typical client systems are: (1) an individual organization; (2) a combination of organizations and agencies under the predominant leadership of one of them; and (3) a combination of agencies of approximately equal status and commitment in the project.

The client system might also possibly be conceived as the entire community, defined as the total aggregate of people and organizations interacting within the geographical area in which the project has relevance—*the community system*.

The client system might also be conceived as one of the three types of organizational structure indicated above—*the project system*. Or again, it might be taken to be the specific organization which is set up to conduct the study itself—*the study system*. Generally speaking, the project system has policy-making functions, while the study system has executing functions. Both the project and study systems develop within an environment of already existing social systems. Of these, the project system seems the most appropriate unit for consideration in the projects under discussion here.

The project system in social research action episodes develops and changes in structure and function with the progression of the project. This change can be analyzed as a sequence of stages involving: (1) the initial systemic environment; (2) the inception of the project system; (3) the expansion of the project system; (4) the operation of the expanded project system; and (5) the transformation of the project system.

As the project system develops, it usually requires expansion both to implement the study design and to incorporate elements that can legitimate the project in the eyes of the appropriate individuals and units of the community. Expansion for execution involves principally the study system; expansion for legitimation usually involves the project system. Such legitimation is best considered to be a continuing process.

Several "fates" may be envisaged for the termination of the project system: (1) it may establish itself as a permanent organization with a program that includes implementing the study's findings; (2) it may simply disband on the completion of its *ad hoc* project; (3) it may seek to establish another more permanent action system, and then dissolve; (4) it may have antedated the research episode and may continue to exist in substantially the same form when the episode is completed. All possibilities were embodied in one or another SRS consultation episode.

Research projects are properly considered to be social action episodes, even when no "implementation" ensues.

Goal Setting and Goal Displacement

Goal setting may be regarded not only as the establishment of a specified set of presumably desirable activities to be carried out, but also a specification of the purposes that these activities are expected to further.

In the SRS experience, the explicit goals that emerged came out of a process of successive attempts at goal formulation and testing of these formulations against the experience of the first year. Thus the goals of the project were not *a priori*, existing independent of the experience which the project provided, nor were they *ex post facto* attempts to place a value-floor under what had already occurred.

Rather, goals directed experience but at the same time experience modified the goals in the direction of "fit" between what one really found oneself doing and the verbalization of the values that determined these choices.

The seven goals of the project involved the promotion of the client organization's growth in effectiveness through:

1. Encouraging careful research as a basis for program planning and operation.

2. Encouraging action in implementing the studies involved.

3. Helping the client organizations acquire a greater awareness of the behavioral components of their work.

4. Helping the client organizations improve their general position in the community.

5. Devising tools, methods, and procedures which might be useful elsewhere in New York State and in other parts of the country.

6. Obtaining study findings which would have program implications elsewhere in New York State and in other parts of the country.

7. Encouraging the utilization of research in health and welfare organizations and agencies throughout New York State and in other parts of the country.

In field consultation on the individual project level, the first encounter of the consultant with the client system usually involved an exploratory process in which it was attempted to formulate the goals of the project, and to assess whether or not there was sufficient convergence of interests between the client's purposes and the overall goals of the SRS.

At the outset of a project relationship, it is advantageous to be explicit about the nature of the project, its goals, methods, the relation of the consultant to it, the structure of the project system, and other pertinent factors. All these matters can be modified or redefined if advisable, but in order to avoid misconceptions and conflicting interpretations of the relationship, they should be stated as clearly as possible at the outset.

Goal displacement involves the substitution of other goals, often those of the system itself or of its constituent members, for the explicit goals which the system purportedly is serving.

Pressures toward goal displacement in the interests of an organization are counterpoised, in the case of a behavioral scientist, by important professional ties and reference-group orientations that afford a different set of standards for "showing results."

Three types of goal displacement pressure are relevant to the behavior of the research consultant: (1) the tendency toward growth in numbers, space, budget, and so on of the research organization (empire-building); (2) the pressure toward showing results in terms of the surrounding organization's needs, but at the sacrifice of more important, more relevant goal attainment; and (3) the substitution of the consultant's own research or career interests for those of the organization he purportedly is serving.

The second type yielded the greatest pressure toward goal displacement in the SRS demonstration.

Goal displacement of this type—showing results in terms of the surrounding organization's needs—in turn involves two subtypes. Type A involves giving inordinate weight to one goal at the expense of one or more of the others, usually of higher priority. Type B substitutes goals other than the seven specified, or substitutes the appearance of goal attainment for actual goal attainment.

Since in this type of consultative relationship, many of the goals are valued instrumentally as a means toward promoting the client organization's growth in effectiveness, Type A goal displacement may arise when these goals become ends in themselves.

Type B goal displacement is particularly relevant for research consultation activities like those of the SRS, since often the appearance of accomplishment, particularly of the first three goals, may be mistaken by the client organizations for actual accomplishment of the goals; or in some cases it may even be preferred by them. In addition, actual accomplishment is likely to cause more inconvenience and be more disruptive.

The pressure of routine and the desire for easy answers or quick results may combine with other pressures to deflect the staff behavioral scientist from bona fide research consultation while he pursues other, more immediately rewarding activities. Examples are: making speeches, sitting in on discussions, preparing memoranda, and other busy-work which can offer the aura of behavioral science through means other than productive endeavor.

Both goal setting and goal displacement may take place at all stages in the development of a project.

Goal Attainment and Goal Failure

In demonstrations of this type, an indication of general goal attainment or failure is the decision of the organization as to whether or not to continue the activity beyond the demonstration period as an integral part of its structure and function.

While the SRS was clearly "successful" on this criterion, a more exacting appraisal calls for the estimation of success or failure as a matter of degree, rather than a dichotomized all-or-none judgment.

A framework for such assessment is provided by an analysis that applies the concepts of goal attainment and goal failure to each of the seven specified goals.

In such an analysis, it becomes apparent that: (1) some goals were given a higher priority than others; (2) some degree of goal failure and goal attainment was experienced with respect to all of the seven goals; and (3) goal attainment and goal failure were more a process than an episodic result.

There are two considerations pertinent here: the extent to which specific activity was directed at the accomplishment of each of these goals, and the extent to which such activity was effective in their accomplishment.

Analysis of our activity provides indication of moderate, but tangible accomplishment of all seven goals, as well as clear indication of failure of full accomplishment in all cases.

In connection with the specific goal of helping the client organizations acquire a greater awareness of the behavioral components of their work, an analysis of the experience indicates little planned, deliberate activity in this respect. Although this goal was explicit, there was no rational strategy to pursue it, but rather there was simply what seemed to be appropriate behavior as specific situations arose. Results, likewise, were modest.

Though goal attainment or failure is not completely under the control of the consultant, there are many situations in which he can take the initiative in furthering a particular goal or set of goals in relation to a project, or refrain from doing so. When should he increase or decrease his initiative in a certain project with respect to one goal or another? Two types of distinction are relevant to this question:

1. In some situations, taking the initiative in order to accomplish a particular goal in a project may not be consistent with the research consultant role as developed earlier in this book. In terms of the seven explicit goals, this usually involves the pursuit of one goal at the expense of another, or of one or more goals at the expense of helping the organization grow in effectiveness.

2. Even where the taking of greater initiative by the consultant would not violate the role conception outlined here, there is usually the matter of available time. With such time limitations, some instances of desirable initiative will be forgone merely because of lack of time. Where this is the case, it is necessary to decide how best to use the time that is available. This, in turn, calls for a consideration of priorities among the seven goals.

While no systematic attempt was made to assign priorities to all the goals, it was understood from the beginning that the first two goals would have highest priority, but always in relation to the purpose of promoting the client organization's growth in effectiveness.

This report of the SRS demonstration has been oriented to two important conceptions. The first is the conception of the research consultant that has been proposed. It is not the only possible conception, nor is it even the usual one, but it is appropriate for research consultation with voluntary citizens' groups in the situations in which the writer was involved. It is a conception that frankly assumes more responsibility toward the client organization than is involved simply in providing technical information and opinions on research design and methodology. The conception is restated here:

The research consultant is a professional person acting in relationship with a client organization, who attempts to promote the organization's growth in effectiveness of structure and function through the utilization of research as a methodology for gaining valid knowledge about the program aspects of the organization's environment and as a dynamic social process that will induce adaptation and change within the organization.

The foregoing conception provides the basis for a second, namely, the importance of the analysis of the project system, and of research projects as action episodes. *For if the research consultant is to honor his obligation to the client organization, as well as to behavioral science and research methodology, he must not only be aware of the need for conceptual analysis of the social process in which he and the client system are involved, but must develop the social interaction skills which this dynamic conception of the research consultation demands.* Although neither of these additional demands on the consultant is easy to fulfill, progress in this direction will be furthered by a growth in the interest which the behavioral scientist attaches to the social processes in which he himself becomes involved as he acts in a consulting capacity.

APPENDICES

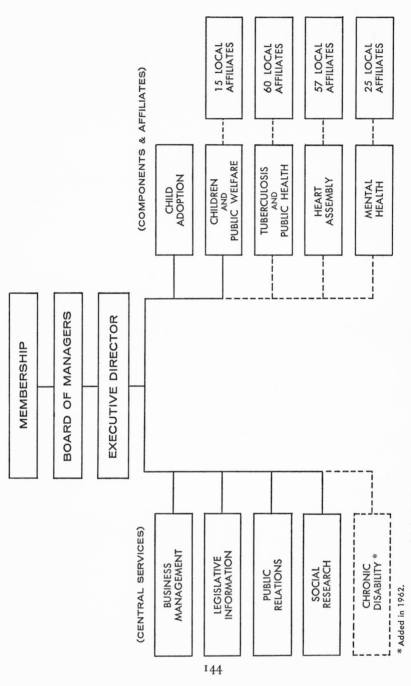

ORGANIZATION OF THE STATE CHARITIES AID ASSOCIATION IN 1960

(COMPONENTS & AFFILIATES)

CHILD ADOPTION

CHILDREN AND PUBLIC WELFARE — 15 LOCAL AFFILIATES

TUBERCULOSIS AND PUBLIC HEALTH — 60 LOCAL AFFILIATES

HEART ASSEMBLY — 57 LOCAL AFFILIATES

MENTAL HEALTH — 25 LOCAL AFFILIATES

MEMBERSHIP

BOARD OF MANAGERS

EXECUTIVE DIRECTOR

(CENTRAL SERVICES)

BUSINESS MANAGEMENT

LEGISLATIVE INFORMATION

PUBLIC RELATIONS

SOCIAL RESEARCH

CHRONIC DISABILITY *

* Added in 1962.

APPENDIX A: Purposes of the State Charities Aid Association as Set Forth in the Currently Effective Certificate of Incorporation

1. To aid and promote the improvement of the mental, moral and physical conditions of the residents of all public charitable institutions in the State;

2. To aid directly, or through its local committees, in the care of destitute adults and dependent and other children needing care, by placing them in families and by exercising an oversight over those who have been placed in families; and by such other methods as from time to time may seem to be desirable;

3. To induce the adoption by the community at large of such measures in the organization and administration of both public and private charity as may develop the self-respect and increase the power of self-support of those receiving help from public or private charity;

4. To stimulate and promote public interest in, and support of, programs designed to better the mental and physical health of the people of the State.

APPENDIX B: Projects on the County, Community, and State Levels

Projects on the County and Community Levels

Epidemiological Study of Tuberculosis Patients. In a county with a relatively high tuberculosis rate, the Tuberculosis and Health Association initiated a committee of relevant officials to consider the problem. The SRS was asked to confer with this committee, as was a behavioral scientist from the State Health Department.

As a first step, it was decided to gather demographic data on all known tuberculosis cases over a five-year period. Pertinent data were selected from the health roster, transferred to punch cards, tabulations prepared of the distribution of the tuberculous population as to age, sex, place of residence, and so on. The analysis was directed by the SRS and turned over to the committee for formulation of program recommendations.

County Mental Health Surveys. A county mental health association had appointed a committee to gather data that could be presented to the County Board of Supervisors in support of setting up of a County Mental Health Board. Such boards receive grant-in-aid funds from the state. The SRS was requested to help in formulating the study design.

Anticipating that there might be similar requests from other mental health associations, the SRS developed a design that would make use of readily available data and the talents of knowledgeable lay citizens, and involve a minimum of financial expenditure. It was further designed so that individual tasks were broadly distributed, and so that analysis and report preparation could be made by the citizens' group itself with a modicum of professional supervision.

Two other mental health associations and three other counties utilized the Survey Guide that was developed, and engaged the SRS in varying consulting capacities.

Screening Device for "Multi-Problem" Families. An urban relocation committee in a large metropolitan county was interested in developing an operationally useful definition of multi-problem families, as well as a screening device to facilitate their selection from agency caseloads. In this effort the SRS aided a committee of social workers, agency officials, and local sociologists in the construction of a measurement scale.

After pretesting, the scale was applied "blind" to 50 multi-problem families from agency caseloads according to a conventional definition, and to 50 families not considered multi-problem. The predictive value of the scale was assessed, and it was to be revised on the basis of an item analysis. Instructions were to be prepared for its wider use.

Evaluating a Program for Multi-Problem Families. A Council of Social Agencies had appointed an interagency "Difficult-Case Committee" to study the problem of persistently dependent families. It wanted to test a program of intensive casework and close interagency collaboration to see whether such a program should become a permanent part of the county's social services.

In a series of consultations with the SRS, a rigorous experimental design was developed. It involved determining multi-problem families according to an operationally precise definition, and the random selection from this universe of a demonstration group and a control group. The experimental variable was intensive casework care with smaller caseload. Ordinary Public Welfare assistance was used for the control. Three independent "before" and "after" measures were applied to ascertain the amount of difference over two years' treatment. Internal analysis of the demonstration group also will be made to see how different types of families may have been changed.

Study of Characteristics of Health Service Recipients. In conjunction with the State Health Department, the SRS developed a project to compare, during a given study year, the demographic characteristics of recipients of public health service such as clinics, public health nursing visits, and the like with the characteristics of the general population. The objective was to see whether the services of the agencies are reaching the types of people their program objectives call for.

A city was found in which the health commissioner and the Tuberculosis and Health Association were willing to organize the project, and where other agencies were willing to participate. Each agency prepared a statement describing the ways in which the recipients of its service should differ, if at all, from the distribution of the general population. Data were then gathered for approximately 20,000 recipients of 18 health services, and each recipient group was compared with the total population by age, sex, census tract, years of schooling, race, national background, employment status, and socioeconomic status. Analyses were to be made by a behavioral scientist in the State Health Department and the SRS. A report was to be furnished each agency showing its actual versus intended target achievements.

Study of County Health Services. A district health officer had enlisted the support of an *ad hoc* citizens' group in making a study of health services. The SRS assisted in the selection of a probability sample of county residents and later in the analysis of the findings. After the survey had been completed, the SRS also furnished consultation to public health nurses who had been assigned to implement the study's findings.

Identifying Tuberculosis Patients Who Are Likely to Become Recalcitrant. The executive secretary of a local health association was concerned with noncooperative tuberculosis patients. Discussions led to the designing of a questionnaire to help identify, shortly after initial diagnosis, patients who are likely to be noncooperative with medical care and thus require special attention. Hypotheses were drawn from analysis of the literature, and plans made to administer this schedule of questions to all newly diagnosed cases in the county for a period of a year.

Evaluating a Mental Health Rehabilitation Program. The Mental Health Association in a large suburban county developed a rehabilitation program for patients who had been released from mental hospitals. It provided daily activities in vocational rehabilitation, home economics, and recreation. In connection with seeking funds, the question arose regarding an evaluation of the program's effectiveness. Several consulting sessions were held to arrive at a research design which could produce valid conclusions regarding the program's effectiveness.

In addition to the foregoing projects, each of which made a major demand on the time of the SRS, others involved one to several consultations. To indicate their scope, the following are listed briefly.

Community Study of the Aged. Consultation on sampling procedures and in the construction of a questionnaire.

Respiratory Diseases Screening Study. Help in constructing a study design and developing data-gathering instruments.

Assessment of Need for Services for Alcoholics. Consultation with an inter-agency committee on possible methods of gathering data.

Study of Parent Refusal to Give Permission for Child's Tuberculin Test. Consultation on design of the study and formulation of the question-naire.

Evaluating the Effectiveness of a Hospital Outpatient Rehabilitation Facility. Consultation on methods of studying the cost and effectiveness of the program.

Study of Agency Utilization of a Social Service Exchange. Help in developing a study design and formulation of data-gathering instruments.

Assessment of a Children's Home with a Declining Community Demand. Con-sultation with the Board of Trustees regarding the possibility of a countywide study of child welfare needs to assess the institution's future role.

Program Implications in a County Health Study. Discussions with community health agencies of the action possibilities from a countywide health study.

A Countywide Rehabilitation Program. Consultation with an interagency committee of the Council of Social Agencies in a small county regarding types of data which might be gathered to help it plan rehabilitation services.

A County's Hospital Needs. Consultation with hospital administrators and county health officials on the implications of available statistics on present hospital facilities and possible future needs.

Emphysema Study. Conferences with a research committee of physicians on the design of an epidemiological study of emphysema in a large institutional population.

A County Long-Term Illness Survey. Consultation with an interagency committee in a large suburban county, to develop a major survey of its long-term illness facilities and needs.

The Educational Impact of a Tuberculin Testing Program. Help in the design of a control-group study to test the retention of a tuberculin-testing program in a city school.

Projects on the State Level

In addition to the foregoing projects on the county and community levels, a number of projects were undertaken on the state level, either on behalf of the State Charities Aid Association or of one of its affiliated statewide organizations.

County Health and Welfare Needs. In conference with the executive director, his deputy, and the Long-Range Planning Committee of SCAA, a proposal was made that the SRS conduct a survey of officials of voluntary and public agencies in the 57 upstate New York counties to ascertain what they considered their greatest health and welfare needs.

The study attempted to appraise three kinds of need: (a) for new or additional services in the health, mental health, and welfare fields beyond what is now available; (b) for additional interagency collaboration; (c) for additional fact finding.

A list of 33 items related to agency services was compiled and a questionnaire developed and pretested in two counties. Single disease entities were excluded as were other items that might be considered the sole concern of a single agency or government department.

The questionnaire was sent to 345 health and welfare leaders in every upstate county; 194 were filled out and returned.

Two fields of need were highest in mentions. These were the chronically ill and the aging, and psychiatric services.

The high items in the "chronic illness-aged" field were: home care services for the chronically ill, rehabilitation services, health services for the aged, public or private infirmaries for the chronically ill, and boarding homes for the aged. The high items relating to "psychiatric services" were: adult psychiatric clinics, services or facilities for emotionally disturbed children, child guidance clinics, services or facilities for mentally retarded children, and expansion of tax-supported mental health activities.

Findings were published by the SCAA under the title *Health and Welfare Needs in New York State:* How 194 Upstate Agency Leaders Appraise Requirements in Their Counties. This study was to become the basis two years later for the addition to the services of the SCAA of a five-year Chronic Disability Program, financed by a $200,000 grant from several foundations.

"Youth in Custody" Studies. Prior to the inception of the SRS, the State Committee on Children and Public Welfare had conducted a study on

the "Treatment of Youths in Upstate New York Local Courts." The SRS suggested that the Committee might wish to make a study of the number of youths under twenty-one in county jails, and to gather data on whether they were awaiting trial or serving sentence, their age, sex, time of offense, length of stay in jail, and so on. It devised a form for recording this material directly from the official county jail rosters. Committees in 12 counties combed the rosters for all entries occurring within the study year. Tabulations and analyses were prepared by the state staff with consultation from the SRS and were published under the title *Youth in Custody*, Part I, A Survey of Minors in Jails in 12 Upstate New York Counties.

At the same time, the SRS agreed to assemble in one publication a listing of the services and facilities dealing with juvenile delinquents in upstate New York. As data were gathered, certain interdepartmental aspects of the configuration of services became apparent. Recommendations drawn up by the SRS and approved by the State Committee on Children and Public Welfare became the basis for the Committee's subsequent program development.

Adoptability Study. The Child Adoption Service of the SCAA had for some time been concerned about children in boarding homes and institutions who might be adoptable, but were not being moved toward adoption placement. With a special grant of funds, it engaged a qualified caseworker to study the adoptability of a sample of 100 children in foster care. The SRS gave extensive consultation to this project. A detailed schedule was developed, pretested, and utilized to extract desired data from case records. Analyses were made of the adoptability status of the children at the time of initial placement with an agency, two years later, and at the time of the study. Findings were published in 1962 by the Child Adoption Service under the title *Adoptability: A Study of 100 Children in Foster Care.*

Statewide Adoption Survey. In conjunction with the State Association of Councils and Chests, the SCAA agreed to survey the practices of agencies and professional people relating to the adoption of children in New York State. A State Committee on Adoption was formed from professional and voluntary agency leaders which became the policy body for the survey. Adoption committees were formed at the county level.

From the beginning, this project was a study-action project, with the findings to serve as basis for program development and possible legislative recommendations. With foundation financial support, a professional staff was engaged both to make the study and to provide field service to the local adoption committees. Instruments were developed and pretested for gathering data from the courts, adoption agencies, hospitals, and from professional organizations of attorneys, physicians, and clergy. Tabulated findings were prepared for each county, the six state welfare districts, and for the state as a whole. These tabulations were presented to the State Committee on Adoption which drew up appropriate recommendations, and issued the report, *Facts to Build On: A Study of Adoption in New York State.*

Multi-Problem Families. Several community planning executives expressed interest in a summary of studies among "multi-problem families" in New York State. It also could help the SRS develop an outline of needed research in this problem area. The SRS therefore compiled a unified précis of all known projects and added an attempted clarification of the concept of multi-problem families in relation to agency programs. It was published under the title *Multi-Problem Families: A New Name or A New Problem?*

County Profiles. Because of general interest in a parallel compilation of basic statistical data for all counties in New York State, the SRS assembled 54 different items and indices for each county, and published the result as *County Profiles: A Compilation of Statistical Items Indicative of Population Characteristics, Economic Factors, and Health and Welfare Conditions of New York State Counties.*

When figures became available from the 1960 Census for incorporated places of 10,000 and over in New York State, *County Profiles* was expanded and revised to form a document that was published in May, 1961, under the title *County and City Profiles.*

Social Research Conference. To support and encourage the utilization of social research in the health and welfare field by other agencies throughout the state, the SRS developed an invitational conference in June, 1960, on the topic "Social Research in the Development of Health and Welfare Agency Programs." Approximately 60 agency administrators and social researchers were invited who had either actual experience in social research in an agency setting, or were contemplating engaging in this work. The program was designed to explore types of problems which arise when social research is conducted in agency settings and in relation to agency programs. Administrators and research persons were invited to present papers and to participate in discussion. The conference proceedings were published in April, 1961, under the title *Social Research in Health and Welfare Agencies*.

Christmas Seal Study. Over the years, the New York State Committee on Tuberculosis and Public Health had extended its activities beyond tuberculosis and respiratory diseases to encompass broader areas of health concern. It was interested in determining the attitudes of givers toward the expanded activities of the local Christmas Seal organizations. The SRS offered extensive consultation to a social scientist who had been engaged for the study.

Research in College Health Education Programs. The SRS was invited to attend a college health education conference sponsored by the State Committee on Tuberculosis and Public Health, and to draw up recommendations for areas of research that could be carried on by the colleges. This developed into a paper presented at the Annual Conference of the State Committee on Tuberculosis and Public Health, and a similar paper presented at the Annual Meeting of the Upstate New York Sociological Society.

APPENDIX C: Publications of the Social Research Service, State Charities Aid Association

Youth in Custody: Facilities for Juvenile Delinquents and Young Offenders in Upstate New York. State Committee on Children and Public Welfare and Social Research Service, January, 1959.

Viewpoint, Social Research Issue, Spring, 1959.

County Profiles, Social Research Service, January, 1959; *County and City Profiles,* May, 1961.

Health and Welfare Needs in New York State: A Survey Report—How 194 Upstate Agency Leaders Appraise Requirements in Their Counties. Social Research Service, January, 1960.

Multi-Problem Families: A New Name or A New Problem? Social Research Service, May, 1960.

Guide for a County Mental Health Survey. Social Research Service, July, 1960.

Social Research in Health and Welfare Agencies: Proceedings of an Invitational Conference on "Social Research in the Development of Health and Welfare Agency Programs," June, 1960.

Published Writings of Author During the Study Period

"Social Research and Community Policy," *International Review of Community Development,* no. 4, 1959.

"Group Autonomy and Community Development," *Autonomous Groups,* vol. 15, nos. 1 and 2, Autumn and Winter, 1959–1960.

"A Note on the T-Group as an Autonomous Group," *Autonomous Groups,* vol. 15, nos. 3 and 4, Spring and Summer, 1960.

"Community Patterns and Community Development," *Merrill-Palmer Quarterly,* vol. 7, no. 4, October, 1961.

The Community in America. Rand McNally and Co., Chicago. In preparation.[1]

[1] Published in 1963.

APPENDIX D: Papers Presented by Author at Scientific or Professional Conferences During the Study Period

"Toward a Theory of Community Development," Society for the Study of Social Problems, August 27, 1960.

"Community Action Patterns," Harvard University, School of Public Health, March 2, 1961, and March 6, 1962; Brandeis University, March 6, 1962.

"Utilizing Research in Legislative Action," National Conference on Social Welfare, Atlantic City, June 8, 1960.

"Communicating with Our School Community," Conference of New York State Association of Elementary Principals, December 5, 1960.

"Opportunities and Resources for Health Research on the County Level," Annual Meeting, New York State Committee on Tuberculosis and Public Health, April, 1960, and Upstate New York Sociological Society, April, 1960.

"Researcher and Administrator: Some Observations on the Relationship," State Charities Aid Association Research Conference, June 16, 1960.

"Value Assumptions in Community Development Activities," Upstate New York Sociological Society, May 6, 1961.

"Research Demonstration of Casework Services to Chronically Dependent Multi-Problem Families: Report of the Chemung County (Elmira) N. Y. Project." Social Research Section, National Conference on Social Welfare, May 30, 1962—with Jesse Smith.

"Who Receives Health Services—Those for Whom They Are Designed or Others: The Demographic Characteristics of Health Service Recipients in an Upstate City." New York State Health Conference, June 11, 1962—with Dr. Walter E. Boek.

APPENDIX E: Speeches by Author During the Study Period

"Community Self-Surveys Without Paid Staff," Columbia University Health Conference, October 1, 1959, and January 28, 1960.

"A Sociologist's Views on Tuberculosis in This Decade," Ulster County Teaching Institute for Nurses, October 7, 1960.

"How Health Officials Compare with Other Local Officials in Assessing County Needs," New York State Health Conference, Behavioral Science Section, May 25, 1960.

"Fact-Finding: Local Opportunities and Resources," State Committee on Tuberculosis and Public Health, 1960 Spring Conference, April 27, 1960.

"Urban Renewal and Socially Handicapped Families," Newburgh Community Service Conference, December 7, 1958.

"Have the Children Changed or Have We?" New York State Welfare Conference, November 18, 1958.

"Multi-Problem Families: Some Answers and Some Questions," New York State Welfare Conference, 1960.

"New Light on an Old Issue: Restoring Multi-Problem Families," State Committee on Children and Public Welfare, Fall Workshop, Johnstown, September 23, 1958; Geneseo, September 18, 1958.

"Tuberculosis—in Focus and Perspective," Ulster County Tuberculosis and Health Association, Annual Meeting, April 28, 1960.

"How to Interest People in What They Don't Want to Know," Cortland County Health Association, Annual Meeting, May 4, 1959.

"Social and Cultural Aspects of Smoking," Empire State Health Council Conference, Albany, February 2, 1961.

"Multi-Problem Families: A New Name or A New Problem?" Seneca County Children's Committee, Annual Meeting, May 21, 1959.

"Services to Multi-Problem Families," Westchester County Council, November, 1958.

"Mutual Interests of Rural and Urban Women," Metropolitan Branch, Women's National Farm and Garden Association, April, 1959.

"Research on Multi-Problem Families," United Community Chest and Council of Onondaga County, Syracuse, April 25, 1961.

"Community Structure and Function," Empire State Health Council Conference, Albany, January 10, 1962.

INDEX

Index